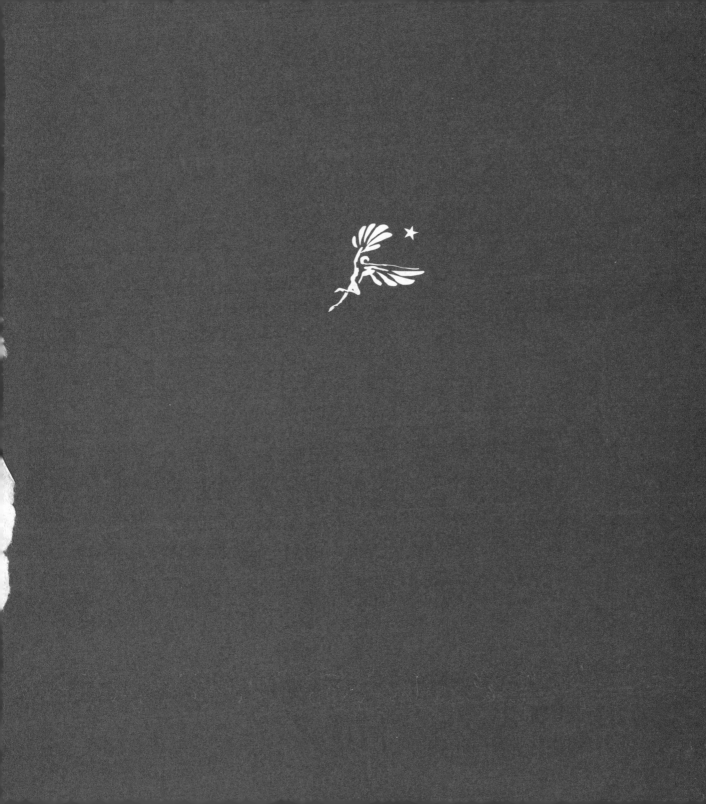

LONG MAY

A TOUCHSTONE BOOK
Published by Simon & Schuster

New York   London   Toronto · Sydney

all. things. running.

YOU RUN

CHRIS COOPER

Touchstone
A Division of Simon & Schuster, Inc.
1230 Avenue of the Americas
New York, NY 10020

First Touchstone hardcover edition October 2010

Touchstone and colophon are registered trademarks of Simon & Schuster, Inc.

For information about special discounts for bulk purchases,
please contact Simon & Schuster Special Sales at 1-866-506-1949
or business@simonandschuster.com.

The Simon & Schuster Speakers Bureau can bring authors to
your live event. For more information or to book an event
contact the Simon & Schuster Speakers Bureau at 1-866-248-3049
or visit our website at www.simonspeakers.com.

Designed by Ruth Lee-Mui

Manufactured in the United States of America

1   3   5   7   9   10   8   6   4   2

Library of Congress Cataloging-in-Publication Data
Cooper, Chris (Christopher Scott)
Long may you run   /   by Chris Cooper.
p.   cm.
"A Touchstone Book."
1. Running—Miscellanea.   2. Running—Training.   3. Physical fitness.
I. Title.
GV1061.5.C68   2010
796.42—dc22   2010024801

ISBN 978-1-4391-9387-7
ISBN 978-1-4391-9424-9 (ebook)

for jin

CONTENTS

PART III:
GET THE GEAR   87

PART IV:
GO THE DISTANCE   113

FOREWORD

"Long May You Run" is not just a great song and a great title for a book about running, it's a great metaphor for life. We all know that running can have enormous health benefits, physically and mentally. In addition, some of the best experiences of my life occurred when I was running. Of course, running in the 2008 Beijing Olympics was a career pinnacle and unforgettable. But I've found that it's often the small, day-to-day aspects of running that are the most precious to me.

I remember my friend and me running 100 laps around the parking lot after high school wrestling practice each week, in frigid temperatures, trying to get that edge on our future opponents. The book you are about to read explains many different and sometimes unique ways of running faster and farther to get better and stronger that will help keep you motivated as well.

I recall stopping with my teammate Steve at a store to buy ice cream sandwiches midrun during track practice. We really thought we needed a boost, and we were sure that ice cream was the best option. In retrospect, perhaps we could have found a healthier alternative! You'll find good advice on fueling and refueling in this book.

Another time I remember coming home from Stanford on a red-eye after running the 10K more than a minute faster than my best time to qualify for the NCAA meet. I was thrilled with my performance, but the long trip put me behind schedule on my training. My teammate Matt got out of bed that morning at 1 a.m. to ride his bike and keep me company while I caught up on my mileage for the week. One of the many essays in this book is about finding someone to run with. For me it made that run so much more enjoyable than doing it alone.

Further along in my running career, I remember how clear and calm the night was and how the moon lit our way during a run over the rural dirt roads of Pennsylvania. I also recall waking up on January 1, 2000, and thinking about how still, peaceful, and sunny it was—even though many people were predicting the end of the world due to Y2K! My runs each of those days were particularly memorable, and they link well with the essays in this book about running under a full moon, enjoying some early-morning runs, and running on New Year's Day.

A few years later, I remember the hot and humid 20-mile run in the orange groves of Florida, just a week before the Boston Marathon, that I was convinced would ruin my chances of running well at that race. Fortunately I went on to place fourth at Boston. In May 2007, I was training intensely for the upcoming 25K U.S. National Championships when my wife and I had our first baby. I remember how proud I felt to be a new dad, and the thought of my new baby's face kept me going during an agonizing 18-miler that day. I went on to win that 25K race later that month. Topics on qualifying for the Boston Marathon, going for a personal record, and race strategies are all additional ways in which this book advises and challenges runners of all ages and abilities. And now maybe I need to check out this book's "Running Behind a Baby Stroller" section more closely . . .

Even short runs have their moments. Just the other day, I saw a coyote cross the road in front of me in the moonlight, and I found myself hoping that I could call on some "get down" speed that I haven't used since college, in case he decided to turn around. It made me think of the time I almost outran a vicious dog in Ecuador (but ended up having to get a series of rabies shots, since he nabbed a piece of my leg before I could get away!). I wished then that I was more Carl Lewis than Bill Rodgers, and I wish I would have read the section in this book dedicated to avoiding dog bites.

Recently I have had to accept the fact that my competitive running career may be over. With two kids, a job, bills, and a house to maintain, every run is a treasure, even if it is only an easy 4-miler. To make a long story short, running is so much more than a great way to feel good and get in shape. It can be a source of many pleasant lifelong memories as well. This book is a great source of motivation, facts, tips, and stories that can help in your quest for your next big marathon—or just get you out the door on your way to another memorable run.

Brian Sell, U.S. Olympic marathoner

INTRODUCTION

Although I have competed in races from the mile to the Boston Marathon, run in foreign countries, on beautiful beaches, through National Parks, and across the Golden Gate Bridge, my running life was lacking something: a good book. Sure, there are many good running books already out there, but I wanted a book that would keep me turning the pages to learn things about running I never knew. One that would help me fill the gaps in my running career, challenge me, and also make me chuckle once in a while. A book that would keep me coming back to it whenever I needed the inspiration of a swift kick in the butt.

That is why I wrote this one—with a little help from nineteen world-class runners and authors. Inside you will discover a whimsical and enlightening collection of nearly 200 topics ranging from training advice and statistics to resolutions and achievable running goals, plus other types of good-to-know information for enhancing the experiences and enjoyment of runners of all ages and abilities. Among other things, you will learn the *one* road race everybody needs to run; how you can win a race even when finishing last; the "destination" runs every runner needs to experience; where to find a luxury ocean cruise just for runners; what to do with your old running shoes and race T-shirts; how listening to the right song and using visualization can improve your performance; and how you can "give back" and be a vital part of the running community. You will also find uplifting anecdotes on runners who have overcome personal challenges and detailed information on races from the popular to the obscure and from the fun to the formidable.

Adding to the uniqueness of this book are recommendations and tips that have been contributed exclusively by the elite group of runners and authors listed on the following page, for the purpose of enhancing your lifelong experience as a runner. All of us hope this extraordinary book will help keep your running fresh and inspire you to continue following the passion you have for the sport as long as you live.

CONTRIBUTORS

Nathan Brannen	2008 Olympian in the 1,500; NCAA 800-meter champion
Keith Brantly	1996 Olympic marathoner; 1998 U.S. Marathon champion
Hazel Clark	Five-time U.S. 800-meter champion; 2008 Olympian
Nancy Clark	Internationally known sports nutritionist and nutrition author
Mark Coogan	Three-time U.S. Road Race champion; 1996 Olympic marathoner
Colleen De Reuck	2009 Boston Marathon Masters winner; four-time Olympian
Jeff Galloway	Running coach and bestselling author; 1972 Olympian in the 10K
Suzy Favor Hamilton	Three-time Olympian in the 1,500 meters; motivational speaker
Scott Jurek	Seven-time winner of the Western States 100-Mile Endurance Run
Don Kardong	Senior writer for *Runner's World*; 1976 Olympic marathoner
Greg Meyer	Past winner of the Boston Marathon; former "Distance Runner of the Year"
Steve Moneghetti	Four-time Olympian in the marathon
Pete Pfitzinger	1984 and 1988 Olympic marathoner; coauthor of *Advanced Marathoning*
Pam Reed	Two-time winner of the Badwater Ultramarathon; author of *The Extra Mile*
Brian Sell	2008 Olympic marathoner; U.S. 25K and half marathon champion
John Stanton	Bestselling author and founder of the Running Room
Kathrine Switzer	First woman to officially run the Boston Marathon; author of *Marathon Woman*
Craig Virgin	Two-time world cross-country champion; three-time Olympian in the 10K
Bart Yasso	Known as the "Mayor of Running"; chief running officer of *Runner's World*; author of *My Life on the Run*

PART I   OFF THE STARTING LINE

BORN TO RUN?

A 2004 study by Harvard University anthropologist Daniel Lieberman and University of Utah biologist Dennis Bramble published in *Nature* provides evidence that specific parts of the human anatomy developed because our early ancestors were more likely to survive if they could run long distances.

Some Anatomical Characteristics that Play a Role in Running, According to the Study	Humans	Chimpanzees
An Achilles tendon, which stores and releases mechanical energy like a spring during running	√	
An ability to perspire to avoid overheating	√	
Large, muscular buttocks, critical for stabilization, allowing the body to lean forward at the hip without falling over	√	
Shorter toes and a big toe that is fully drawn in toward the other toes for pushing off during running	√	
Stiff arches that make the feet more rigid for pushing off the ground	√	
Longer legs, which allow longer strides	√	
Shorter forearms, to help the upper body counterbalance the lower body during running	√	
Ability of the upper body to move independently from the lower body to counterbalance fast-moving legs	√	
A ligament that runs from the back of the skull and neck down to the thoracic vertebrae that stabilizes the head when moving at a fast pace	√	
Larger ankle, knee, and hip joints for improved shock absorption	√	
An enlarged heel bone for additional shock absorption	√	
Large vertebrae and disks that allow the back to withstand greater forces as the legs hit the ground	√	

WHY WE KEEP GOING

Our early ancestors ran to eat and avoid being eaten. In what anthropologists call persistence hunting, those early runners pursued four-footed animals over long distances for hours and sometimes days, eventually running their prey to exhaustion. Sprinting shorter distances enabled them to escape hungry predators. We still run, but now we run for different reasons, as you can see in the list below. What's your motivation?

TOP REASONS WE CONTINUE TO RUN

1	To stay in shape		8	To socialize with others
2	To stay healthy		9	To improve state of mind
3	To relieve stress		10	To improve speed or endurance
4	To meet a personal challenge		11	To appreciate nature, scenery
5	To achieve a goal		12	To be alone, solitary
6	To control weight		13	To compete against others
7	To have fun			

Source: From Running USA's 2008 State of the Sport series based on the most recent online National Runner Survey of more than 8,000 active adult runners conducted by Running USA. See www.runningusa.org for more information on survey participants.

HEALTH BENEFITS OF RUNNING

Improves cardiovascular fitness

Raises good HDL cholesterol

Helps relieve stress

Lowers heart rate

Increases bone density

Lowers triglycerides

Helps lower blood pressure

Increases lung capacity

Lowers bad LDL cholesterol

Boosts the immune system

Reduces the risk of stroke

Slows the aging process

Reduces the risk of blood clot formation

Helps maintain a healthy weight

How does running stack up to other sports in terms of calories burned? The chart below shows the approximate number of calories expended *per hour* during various athletic activities.

CALORIES BURNED PER HOUR

Walking slowly	200	Walking briskly	300	Swimming	300–650
Golf	250	Tennis	400–500	Biking (13 mph)	660
Bowling	270	Racquetball	600	Running	800–1,000

For a more accurate reading of the calories you personally expend during a run, you can visit www.webmd.com/diet/healthtool-fitness-calorie-counter. This fitness and exercise calculator will ask you to input your body weight, your estimated pace, and the run's duration in hours and/or minutes, helping you to decide whether to reward yourself with a second helping of Mom's apple pie.

If you subscribe to the philosophy of Deena Kastor, however, you need not worry about the quantity, only the *quality,* of calories. America's fastest women's marathoner told *New York Times* foodie Mark Bittman, "I eat a lot of calories but I don't count calories. I think the beauty and great marriage of running and eating is that you're expending a lot of energy and you need to consume a lot of energy. I do eat everything and anything I want, but what I want is good nutritious food."

If Oprah Can Do It, So Can You

Running is the greatest metaphor for life,
because you get out of it what you put into it.

—Oprah Winfrey

Years ago, Oprah Winfrey weighed more than 200 pounds despite having completed yet another low-calorie/low-fat diet, so she had an exercise physiologist put her on a running program.

After two weeks of mixing jogging and walking, she was able to run up to three miles without stopping. Staying motivated, she was soon rising at 5 a.m. to get in her five to six miles at a 10- to 11-minute pace. Because having a goal in sight helps runners stay focused on their training programs, the doctor prescribed a half marathon race (13.1 miles), which Oprah did a few months later.

By the time she achieved her goal weight of 150 pounds, she could cover five miles at an 8-minute pace. Then she made a key decision every runner should consider: she set another goal. That goal was realized in November 1994, when she completed the Marine Corps Marathon (26.2 miles) in Washington, D.C.

Oprah showed that whether your goal is healthy weight loss, doing a marathon, or just completing one loop around the block, anyone can be a successful runner. All you have to do is believe in yourself.

JOIN A RUNNING CLUB

Many of us love the solitude of running alone, though we still need the encouragement and companionship of other runners as we churn out our weekly mileage. That's why every runner should join a running club.

Local running clubs exist to promote running as a healthy lifestyle choice in the community and are components of a good running program. Like any group, they foster accountability, encouragement, and companionship among members. Typically, running clubs sponsor group training sessions at local tracks, conduct weekly group runs, and inform about upcoming races. They also provide social activities where like-minded individuals can talk openly about mile splits, interval workouts, and blackened toenails without being considered, well, strange. Clubs are especially beneficial for runners who struggle with the motivation to maintain a regular schedule on their own or for those who need running buddies who can push them to train harder than they ever could alone. Writer and Olympian Don Kardong, one of this book's contributors, says that this motivational aspect is the reason he recommends that every runner run with a group at least once a week.

Furthermore, there is evidence that membership in a running group may be better for the brain; at least for rats. A study published in *Nature Neuroscience* examined the effects of running on creating new neurons (a process known as neurogenesis) in the brains of adult rats housed in groups versus those kept in isolation. The authors report that running increased neurogenesis (a positive outcome) only among the rats who were housed in groups; neurogenesis was suppressed in rodents that lived and ran alone, in the absence of social interaction.

Although similar studies have not been conducted among runners of the two-legged variety, several organizations see empirical evidence that living and training in groups can benefit a runner's performance. The Hansons-Brooks Distance Project of Rochester, Michigan, is one of those organizations. Kevin and Keith Hanson saw an opportunity to provide elite runners coming out of college with the motivational (and financial) support to help them advance to the next competitive level, with the Olympics being the ultimate goal. Realizing that countries with great distance-running reputations such as Japan, Kenya, and Ethiopia all emphasized group training, the brothers joined forces with Brooks Running, Inc., to start this program, where athletes are housed together and train together. Brian Sell, a Hansons-Brooks team member and another of this book's contributors, evidently benefited from that group training model by earning a spot on the 2008 U.S. Olympic Marathon team.

U.S. marathoner Kara Goucher is also a believer in group training as it relates to improving performance. In a *New York Times* article titled "To Train Harder, Consider a Crowd," she says she often struggled while training alone after college. After she moved to Oregon and joined a team organized by the running legend Alberto Salazar, she noticed a difference.

> I think it's possible to train on your own, but I do think it's better in a group. You see success in each other. Everything seems within reach.
> —Kara Goucher

Even if your name isn't Brian Sell or Kara Goucher, you can join a running club and reap the benefits of running and training with others. New York Road Runners, for example (www.nyrr .org), is "dedicated to promoting the sport of distance running, enhancing health and fitness for all, and responding to community needs." NYRR serves 40,000 members in the New York City area and has members in all fifty states. Another option is to contact the Road Runners Club of America. The RRCA "is dedicated to supporting the growth of grassroots running clubs, training programs, and running events while promoting the common interests of runners throughout the United States," and claims about 200,000 members. Visit www.rrca.org and click on "Find a Running Club" for the contact information of organized running groups near you. An alternative for mothers is www.seemommyrun.com, a nonprofit networking Web portal that enables moms to locate a running or walking group in their area. Otherwise, your favorite running store is always a good source of information about the local running club scene. And if you can't find a running club near you, why not start your own? Rats shouldn't have all the fun.

THE "DRINKING CLUB WITH A RUNNING PROBLEM"

It is the largest running organization in the world, but you've probably never heard of it. Its members meet in clubs called kennels, refer to one another as hounds or hares, and exist for the enjoyment of exercise, camaraderie, and beer—not necessarily in that order. They are the Hash House Harriers.

Back in 1938, a group of British officers and expats in Malaysia formed a running group and sponsored events called hashes, based on the old English game of Paper Chase or Hare and Hounds. The group's name was a commentary on the food served at their meeting place. The weekly runs were disrupted by the outbreak of World War II but were resumed after peacetime as other groups formed. But it wasn't until the 1960s and '70s that the sport's popularity spread throughout the world. Today, "hashing" is practiced on every continent in nearly 2,000 groups, or kennels, and in every major city on the planet.

According to the charter, the goals of the hash are: (1) To promote physical fitness among our members; (2) To get rid of weekend hangovers; (3) To acquire a good thirst and to satisfy it in beer; and (4) To persuade the older members that they are not as old as they feel.

In hashing, runners called hounds chase after another runner called the hare, who leaves a trail of flour or paper through fields, streams, and woods or, alternatively, through suburban neighborhoods, strip malls, and public parks. The challenge for the hare is to lay a trail that is confusing or difficult to follow, enabling slower runners to catch up to the faster ones at various checkpoints. Indeed, hashing is a noncompetitive sport. A Philadelphia kennel, for example, stipulates that "Speed is not important. If you race, you will be tripped." The hounds' goal is to find the stash of beer and munchies at the end of the trail, which is typically three to six miles in length. Just as rewarding is the opportunity to socialize and observe other traditions of the kennel at the end of each run.

To find the location of the kennel nearest you and more information about the organization, visit www.gotothehash.net.

KEEP A RUNNING LOG

Logging your training runs, workouts, and races should be more than just a way to keep track of your miles. A good running log should be used both retrospectively and prospectively, as a record of past runs and as a way to plan and organize future workouts.

Recording the details of your running workouts provides a means to analyze your training successes as well as those times when things didn't go well. You can see which training regimens worked and which ones didn't; which workouts generated better results without injury and which ones left you feeling as if you may have overtrained. The key word is *details*. Don't record just "seven miles" for Sunday. Include whatever else you think is appropriate for a full appreciation of each training day: the time of day and temperature; how you felt when you awoke that day; the amount of warm-up and stretching you did; what you ate to fuel and to refuel; the effort you expended; the route you took; and any memorable moments, such as seeing a deer on the trail. Most important, record how you felt afterward —both physically and emotionally.

Use your running log as well to plan your training for a future race. With a goal race in mind, work backward from the date when you want to be in peak condition. Pencil in the days for long runs that build endurance (how far) and for speed work on the track (how many repeats). Plan rest days and the dates and routes for your other training runs. Add variety and cross-training, and tweak the log when necessary based on any change in your physical condition or training goals.

Training logs can be anything from a basic calendar to one of the comprehensive bound record books found in bookstores. Alternatively, you can examine the many free running logs and templates available online (such as at www.logthatrun.com or www.runningahead.com) and see which one fits your needs the best.

A *gradual* increase in mileage and intensity is key. I have seen many people start running, feel great after two weeks, push it too hard and try to do something twice as long or far as they have done so far, and get injured or feel dead for the next couple months. It's better to have an average three months than one month great and two months of not running.

—Brian Sell
2008 Olympic marathoner

RUN ACROSS THE UNITED STATES WITHOUT EVER LEAVING HOME

Though not a substitute for a true running log, http://exercise.lbl.gov/index.html enables runners to log their daily mileage and then track their progress on a virtual transcontinental trip across the United States. The site was designed by researchers at the Lawrence Berkeley National Laboratory to encourage runners (and walkers and cyclists) to keep up with their weekly fitness goals.

When you log in and enter your mileage for a particular day, your cumulative total is calculated, and the Web site displays the particular scenery you would observe at that distance—by means of photographs—as a runner leaving from the starting point in Yorktown, Virginia, and continuing west toward the final destination in Florence, Oregon.

For example, if you ran 4 miles one day, 5 the next day, and 6.2 on the third day, you would see photos of the scenery at 4 miles, 9 miles, and 15.2 miles west of Yorktown on days one, two, and three, respectively. The site also provides maps that chart your progress and the progress of your running partner, if you decide to include a friend. In addition, the site can send you an e-mail notification when you don't meet your weekly running goal or when your running partner has a particularly good week and passes you along the route.

A real-life coast-to-coast run took place in 1928. Known as the Bunion Derby, the race took the 199 entrants on a 3,400-mile course from California to New York, much of it along old Route 66. Runners would race between designated towns, after which they would eat, sleep, wake up, and do it all over again the next day. After eighty-four days, a Cherokee from Oklahoma, appropriately named Andy Payne, crossed the finish line first and pocketed the $25,000 winner's prize. An account of the Bunion Derby can be found in the book *C. C. Pyle's Amazing Foot Race: The True Story of the 1928 Coast-to-Coast Run Across America* by Geoff Williams.

SOME CELEBRITY RUNNERS

Robin Williams, comedian

Kim Alexis, model

Katie Holmes, actress

Jeff Corwin, TV host

Sarah Ferguson, Duchess of York

Mario Lopez, actor

Joan Van Ark, actress

Gordon Ramsay, chef

David Petraeus, U.S. Army general

Jay Leno, TV host

Meredith Baxter, actress

Melvin Van Peebles, actor/composer

William Baldwin, actor

Oprah Winfrey, TV host

Will Ferrell, actor

P. Diddy, musician

Emily Procter, actress

David Letterman, TV host

Edward Norton, actor

Ted Corbitt

Many consider Ted Corbitt the father of American distance running. The child who began running on his father's cotton farm in South Carolina eventually found longer distances to his liking and became known for his 200-mile training weeks. He set American records for the marathon, 25, 40, 50, and 100 miles, while helping break the color barrier in competitive running. In his career he ran 199 marathons, including 21 Boston Marathons under three hours, and competed as a member of the 1952 U.S. Olympic team. Corbitt was the founding president of the New York Road Runners and a race organizer who was instrumental in helping road racing gain professional status. His enhanced system of measuring and certifying race courses is still in use today.

THE 25 BEST RUNNING CITIES IN AMERICA

Rank	City	Rank	City
1	San Francisco, California	14	Colorado Springs, Colorado
2	San Diego, California	15	Dallas, Texas
3	New York, New York	16	Anchorage, Alaska
4	Chicago, Illinois	17	Raleigh, North Carolina
5	Washington, D.C.	18	Salt Lake City, Utah
6	Minneapolis–St. Paul, Minnesota	19	Honolulu, Hawaii
7	Boulder, Colorado	20	Atlanta, Georgia
8	Boston, Massachusetts	21	Houston, Texas
9	Denver, Colorado	22	Phoenix, Arizona
10	Portland, Oregon	23	Madison, Wisconsin
11	Austin, Texas	24	Monterey, California
12	Seattle, Washington	25	Fort Collins, Colorado
13	Philadelphia, Pennsylvania		

Source: Based on a *Runner's World* survey of jogging participation, number of running clubs per city, the annual number of road races, the amount of land set aside for park usage, air quality measurements, weather data, crime statistics, and a poll in which readers ranked their favorite running cities.

RUN ON A BEACH

I was exceedingly surprised with the print of a man's naked foot
on the shore, which was very plain to be seen in the sand.

—*Daniel Defoe,* Robinson Crusoe

It is not known if the man belonging to the footprint discovered by Robinson Crusoe had been out for a morning run on that beach, but it's not out of the question. He would have known the joy of running on firm, wet sand that many of us never experience. Greg Meyer was the last American male to win the Boston Marathon in 1983. Keith Brantly competed for the United States in the 1996 Olympic Marathon. Both of these contributors said that taking a run on a beach is something all runners should do at least once in their life, whether it's at Hanalei Bay on the island of Kauai, Coolum Beach along Australia's Sunshine Coast, Malibu in southern California, or the New Jersey shore.

Running on the beach is much easier than attempting to explain why it gives runners such a special feeling, although Sister Marion Irvine, an Olympic Marathon Trials qualifier, comes close: "It's elevating and humbling at the same time," she says in *The Quotable Runner.* "Running along a beach at sunrise with no other footprints in the sand, you realize the vastness of creation, your own insignificant space in the plan, how tiny you really are."

Though beaches and bare feet go together like, well, sun and sunburn, it's better to slip on the running shoes when attempting that early-morning run. That is, if you want a good, brisk workout. Shoes will not only allow you to run faster but will protect feet that are not yet accustomed to an unfamiliar, uneven, and inconsistent surface. In addition, the firm, wet sand at the water's edge requires more cushioning and support for the feet than you would expect, especially when running at a reasonable training pace. Make sure you cover roughly the same distance each way so both legs are equally exposed to the camber of the beach if there is one. You can avoid this upward curve along the shore by running at low tide.

When the urge to run freely without the constraints of shoes and socks becomes too great, enjoy it, but don't overdo it. Begin with just a quarter mile up and back at a slow, easy pace that first day. Until your feet become accustomed to barefoot running, whether on wet sand or soft, you are at greater risk of suffering calf and Achilles tendon strain. Keep in mind that running at the beach, with or without shoes, also provides feedback on your running technique. A review of those footprints in the virgin sand may reveal that you are under- or overstriding, that you are landing on your toes or heels rather than the midfoot, or that your feet are rolling inward or outward with each stride. Just be sure to do this visual inspection before the next big wave washes away any trace that you were ever there.

Finally, don't forget the sunscreen, and avoid being distracted by sunbathers in Speedos and bikinis; something Robinson Crusoe never had to be concerned about.

Use a calendar or PDA to schedule your runs the same way you do business appointments. If you try to run "when you have time," you'll never get it done.

—Don Kardong
Senior writer for *Runner's World*
1976 Olympic marathoner

Some Quotes for Inspiration

Here and throughout the book are quotes that may provide needed inspiration for that long training run, the upcoming race, or just getting out of bed and getting in a run before work. You can also thumb through *Bartlett's Familiar Quotations* or *The Quotable Runner*, surf the Internet, or dig down deep and make up your own. Then stick them on your refrigerator, post them on your bathroom mirror, or write them on your arm before the big race.

"If you want to become the best runner you can be, start now.
Don't spend the rest of your life wondering if you can do it."
—Priscilla Welch

"Everyone benefits from running, both in ways they recognize and
in ways they don't. One thing that almost always happens is
that your sense of self-worth improves.
You accept yourself a little better."
—Ted Corbitt

"To give anything less than your best is to sacrifice the Gift."
—Steve Prefontaine

"The real purpose of running isn't to win a race;
it's to test the limits of the human heart."
—Bill Bowerman

BEST RUNNING MOVIES

1. **Chariots of Fire** (1981)
   This inspiring story of two British athletes who compete in the 1924 Olympics won the Best Picture Oscar. Good acting, well-staged race sequences, and a memorable run on a beach are among the highlights.

2. **Fire on the Track: The Steve Prefontaine Story** (1995)
   A documentary about the cult hero and one of America's best-ever distance runners. This film, which preceded two glossier feature films about Prefontaine, is brought to life by more than 50 storytellers who were not actors but friends and fellow competitors.

3. **Without Limits** (1998)
   This Tom Cruise–produced story of Steve Prefontaine was written by friend and Olympian Kenny Moore and starred Billy Crudup.

4. **Gallipoli** (1981)
   The Peter Weir–directed film about two Aussies (Mel Gibson and Mark Lee) whose running careers are interrupted by Australia's involvement in World War I. Coach: "What are your legs?" Archy: "Springs. Steel springs." Coach: "What are they going to do?" Archy: "Hurl me down the track." Enough said.

5. **Endurance** (1999)
   Director Bud Greenspan's race footage highlights this biography of the Ethiopian runner Haile Gebrselassie, perhaps the greatest distance runner ever.

6. **The Games** (1970)

A look at the personalities and training methods of four distance runners, including an Australian aborigine, as they prepare for and compete in the Olympic Marathon. Ryan O'Neal is the American hopeful with a passion for running and performance-enhancing drugs.

7. **Prefontaine** (1997)

This Disney version of Prefontaine's life starring Jared Leto received "two thumbs up" from Siskel and Ebert.

8. **Marathon Man** (1976)

Distance-running grad student Dustin Hoffman gets mixed up with some bad people. After seeing this, you may not want to visit your dentist ever again.

9. **Running Brave** (1983)

The inspirational story of Native American Billy Mills, who came from obscurity to win gold in one of the biggest upsets in Olympic history.

ENJOY SOME EARLY-MORNING RUNS

Full many a glorious morning I have seen.

—*William Shakespeare*

Not everyone enjoys running early in the morning, probably because not everyone wants to wake up early to go running in the morning. Morning running does have its converts, however. For every ten runners who favor evening or afternoon runs, there's one person who looks forward to rising at 5:45 each day while the rest of us are still cradled in the blissful arms of sleep.

They enjoy being the only one out on the road or the sidewalk or the track as the sun comes up, when all the senses become alive and acute. It's during that peaceful solitude that they can temporarily cast aside the clutter of daily life—e-mail, voice mail, credit card balances, to-do lists, what they didn't say, what they shouldn't have said—and replace it with a joy that comes from doing what they love to do and what they were born to do. Some claim they do their best thinking on those early-morning runs. Others enjoy the adrenaline jolt those runs provide that helps wake them up and jump-start their day. And all are assured of getting in that daily run before a busy schedule interferes with the rest of the day.

Give yourself extra time to warm up on top of what you normally do, since your muscles and joints are stiffer when you first wake up. If you need a goal, try running (rather than driving) to your favorite coffee shop for that morning cup of java. Finally, don't let the exhilaration of an early-morning run on the roads keep you from being vigilant for cars with still-sleepy drivers behind the wheel.

RUNNING IN THE BIBLE (NEW INTERNATIONAL VERSION)

"Come what may, I want to run."—2 Samuel 18:23

"Let us run with perseverance the race marked out for us."—Hebrews 12:1

"I do not run like a man running aimlessly."—1 Corinthians 9:26

"He makes my feet like the feet of a deer."—Psalm 18:33

"Both were running, but the other disciple outran Peter and reached the tomb first."—John 20:4

"Do you not know that in a race all the runners run, but only one gets the prize?"—1 Corinthians 9:24

"They will run and not grow weary."—Isaiah 40:31

"I have fought the good fight, I have finished the race, I have kept the faith."—2 Timothy 4:7

Roger Bannister

Roger Bannister was motivated at a young age to succeed in running in order to win an athletic scholarship to a university whose tuition was otherwise beyond the reach of his working-class parents. At Oxford, he gained elite status in the mile and 1,500 meters but decided against competing in the 1948 Olympics so he could concentrate on his studies. Four years later he went to the Helsinki Olympics, where he finished fourth in the 1,500, a result that motivated him to train even harder.

Then, on May 6, 1954, he became the first person to break the four-minute mile by running the four laps of Oxford's Iffley Road track in a time of 3:59.4. When one considers that the busy medical student lacked the sophisticated training of today's elite athletes, ran the race on a speed-killing cinder track, and could usually spare just 45 minutes a day to train, that accomplishment seems even more extraordinary. Bannister became a neurologist when his track career ended and later became Sir Roger Bannister upon being knighted by the queen in 1975.

YOU KNOW YOU'RE A RUNNER WHEN . . .

You consider pasta a food group.

The theme from *Rocky* gives you goose bumps.

You give up running for Lent.

You have a quilt made from old race T-shirts.

You can easily convert kilometers to miles and vice versa.

Your calf muscles are bigger than your biceps.

You correct others that a marathon is really 26 *point two* miles.

You get a massage, but it's not for pleasure.

You use "easy run" and "five miles" in the same sentence.

You have more shoes than your wife, and they're all for running.

You enjoy going to the golf course, but not to golf.

You're envious when you see runners on the road and you're driving in a car.

You spend more on running clothes than on school or work clothes.

Many of your toenails are not pink anymore.

There is a "running" playlist on your iPod.

You view drinking beer as carbo-loading.

You arrive sooner using the steps than the people taking the elevator.

You run for fun.

If none of these describes you, hopefully they will soon.

After you have a solid base, try picking
up the pace in some of your workouts.
It's a thrill to find yourself improving.

—Kathrine Switzer
First woman to officially run
the Boston Marathon
Author of *Marathon Woman*

PART II   ON THE ROAD

ARE YOU THE TYPICAL RUNNER?

According to the National Runner Survey, the typical distance runner has the following profile:

	Female	Male
Runs 4+ days/week	75%	79%
Average number of miles run per week	23	30
Average number of years running	11	16
Running events entered past year	7	9
Has completed one or more marathons	54%	68%
Favorite race distance	Half marathon	Half marathon
A "frequent/fitness" runner	65%	56%
Runs 12 months a year	80%	82%
Buys shoes at a running specialty store	50%	43%
Graduated from college	79%	79%
Is married	62%	74%

Source: From Running USA's 2009 State of the Sport series based on the most recent online National Runner Survey of more than 11,000 active adult runners compiled by Running USA. See www.runningusa.org for more information on survey participants.

RUNNING AND TRAFFIC

According to the National Highway Traffic Safety Administration (NHTSA), approximately 70,000 pedestrians are injured annually by automobiles, with about 4,600 pedestrian fatalities. While the statistics give no indication of how many of those pedestrians are runners, the message is clear: being safe when running on the roads is much more than just running in the direction against traffic, as we were always taught. Here are some more sobering findings from the book *Traffic: Why We Drive the Way We Do (and What It Says About Us)* by Tom Vanderbilt:

- Pedestrians *think* drivers can see them up to twice as far away as drivers actually do.
- Drivers often have no clue about how fast they are driving. In a study measuring the speed of drivers as they passed children waiting to cross a street, drivers thought they were going at least 12 miles per hour slower than they actually were (i.e., they thought they were going 18 to 25 miles per hour when they were actually doing 30 to 37 miles per hour).
- During night driving, according to one expert, a driver would have to be going no more than 20 miles per hour to ensure seeing every potential hazard in time to stop, including, say, a runner in reflective clothing.
- Most automobile accidents happen very close to home. When drivers enter a familiar setting such as the streets in their neighborhood, habits take over, they let their mental guard down and become less cautious.
- Above 20 miles per hour, drivers begin to lose eye contact with pedestrians, and the chances of a pedestrian dying if hit by a car increase dramatically.

You can go to www.rrca.org for a good list of running safety tips.

WORK ON YOUR FORM

Hal Higdon, in the book *Run Fast,* describes running efficiently and economically as "when you're running at the same speed as your competitor, the pace seems easier to you than it does to him. Or, when you're running with the same effort as your competitor, you're running faster than they are." Much of our capability for running long and running fast comes from an efficient running form, an asset that many of us ignore. Some are born with good running form and mechanics, others not. Even the most inefficient runners, however, can squeeze a few seconds from their 5K times or a few minutes from longer races by making minor modifications to their form for more efficient and effective running.

Generally accepted is that more efficient runners land on the midfoot first (rather than the heel), then drop down on the heel before pushing off with the arch and the toes. One should avoid swinging the arms sideways across the body, and the head should be kept still and looking straight ahead, not at the feet. Beyond that, however, there are many conflicting messages about correct running form.

In *Runner's World Complete Book of Beginning Running,* Amby Burfoot says that running form is "as individual as a fingerprint and is too inborn to change very much." Therefore, he suggests keeping it simple and offers these general guidelines:

- Run "tall" and upright. Don't lean forward, but keep ears, neck, hips, and feet all in the same line, like a marionette or puppet on a string.
- Running faster should be accomplished not by overreaching with each stride but by increasing the rate of your stride turnover.
- Glide over the ground in smooth strides rather than bouncing.
- When running uphill, shorten your stride and drive more with your arms. When going downhill, lean slightly forward and just let gravity do the work for you.

A somewhat different perspective on running form is held by Danny Dreyer, the author of *Chi-Running: A Revolutionary Approach to Effortless, Injury-free Running.* This fairly new running discipline and philosophy is based on the same principles as t'ai chi: working with core muscles and integrating the mind with the body with a focus on performance and well-being. In his book, Dreyer says that efficient and biomechanically correct running "comes from relaxing muscles, opening tight joints, and using gravity to do the work instead of pushing and forcing the body to move in ways that can do it harm." In ChiRunning, the upper body leans forward with the pull of gravity, the foot gently lands with a midfoot strike under the core or "center" (never out in front), the legs are relied upon for support, not propulsion, and cadence or stride turnover never changes; it is the length of the stride that changes your speed.

> "The one easy step every runner can take to improve running form is to be more relaxed when they run."
> —*Running Well*

Caution should be used, however, when tinkering with your form, because too much emphasis on fixing any one element could do more harm than good. If you are often injured or find running painful at times, you should definitely consider addressing your running technique. Otherwise, if you feel comfortable and relaxed when you run, it's best to adopt the "If it ain't broke, don't fix it" philosophy.

Everyone, however, can benefit from a few easy drills that improve coordination, range of motion, and overall technique by exaggerating certain parts of the running gait: strides (as described later in Keith Brantly's running tip), high knees, butt kicks, fast feet, skipping, and crossovers, as well as backward running. These drills can be found in training books or demonstrated in online videos like the one on the *Running Times* Web site.

As with ChiRunning, one word invariably comes up when experts discuss ways of improving running technique: relaxation. The authors of the book *Running Well* advise runners to avoid tension and effort where it is not needed, to achieve more efficient running. "The one easy step every runner can take to improve running form is to be more relaxed when they run." For example, one doesn't need tense shoulders, a clenched jaw or clenched fists, a frowning face, or squinting eyes to aid performance. They add that "running relaxed doesn't mean running slowly. It is something you should be able to maintain whatever your pace."

RUNNING IN DIRTY AIR

Haile Gebrselassie of Ethiopia decided against competing in the Beijing Marathon due to concerns about the poor air quality in the Olympic city. Therefore, based on results from the 2010 *State of the Air* report by the American Lung Association, the distance-running superstar would likely bypass competing in many U.S. cities as well.

The American Lung Association monitors three categories of air pollution for its annual report: ozone, year-round particle pollution, and short-term particle pollution. Looking at the nation as a whole, the report finds that about 6 out of 10 people (175.3 million) in the United States live in counties that have unhealthful levels of either ozone or particle pollution. Below are the cities ranked highest for at least two of the three pollution categories.

U.S. CITIES WITH THE POOREST AIR QUALITY

Atlanta, Georgia	Merced, California
Bakersfield, California	Modesto, California
Birmingham, Alabama	New York, New York/Newark, New Jersey
Cincinnati, Ohio	Philadelphia, Pennsylvania/Camden, New Jersey
Fresno, California	Phoenix-Mesa-Scottsdale, Arizona
Hanford-Corcoran, California	Pittsburgh, Pennsylvania
Houston, Texas	Sacramento, California
Indianapolis, Indiana	San Diego, California
Knoxville, Tennessee	Visalia-Porterville, California
Los Angeles–Long Beach, California	Washington, D.C./Baltimore, Maryland/Northern Virginia

The American Lung Association warns that breathing polluted air can seriously harm your health and even shorten your life. Athletes are especially susceptible to the dangers of air pollution due to the increased amount of air they breathe in and out while running. Commonsense advice on avoiding high levels of air pollution, especially on days when pollution levels are critical, includes the following:

- It is better to run earlier in the day, when heat and pollution levels are at their lowest.
- Cut back on the intensity of your run. If you race on a day with high pollution levels, make it an easy fun run instead of an all-out effort; there will be other days to try for a personal record.
- Find some green space like a park for your runs. Side streets with less traffic are another alternative to busy roads, particularly during evening rush hour.
- Check the U.S. Air Quality Summary at www.airnow.gov for the daily air quality in your area, especially in hot weather. An Air Quality Index (AQI) of 101 to 150 is considered unhealthy for sensitive individuals; above 150 is considered unhealthy for everyone.
- Finally, run inside on a treadmill or ride an exercise bike if conditions are especially bad.

If a Superstar Chef Can Do It, So Can You

The restaurateur and winemaker Joe Bastianich is a part owner of eighteen restaurants in New York, Las Vegas, and Los Angeles along with his mother, the chef Lidia Bastianich, and Mario Batali. For years Joe enjoyed regular marathon eating sessions due to the nature of his job, until a talk with his doctor convinced him to take up running.

"Before, food and wine were the dominating things in my life," he told *The New York Times*. "You do all that and you never worried about the effects because the effects are inherent to the job." Eventually, his passion for overindulgence gave way to a newfound passion for running, with a goal of completing another kind of marathon—the kind that is 26.2 miles long. By following a strict running regimen—mostly morning runs to accommodate his schedule—Bastianich lost 45 pounds from his 248-pound frame and within a year completed the New York City Marathon.

Not one to diet, Bastianich still enjoys good food and wine but moderates his food intake and avoids late-night meals altogether. "The running regimen dictates what you can do," he said in a *GQ* interview. "You can't go out and drink two bottles of wine and run nine miles the next day. The bottom line is, running is part of my lifestyle now. I work out because it makes me feel better, it makes me perform better, it makes my life better."

USE INTERVAL TRAINING

Scientists consider the maximum amount of oxygen that can be delivered to your muscles during exercise to be the most basic measure of aerobic fitness. Technically it's called VO_2 max, but you can just call it "aerobic capacity." Simply put, by increasing the amount of oxygen that can be delivered to and used by your muscles, you can run farther and faster.

One of the most efficient ways to increase your aerobic capacity is through interval workouts on the track. The fictional miler Quenton Cassidy, in the book *Once a Runner,* claims that intervals make a runner "racing mean." These workouts are repetitions run at a measured distance and pace, followed by a rest interval. Typically, the distance for the repetition is 440 yards (one lap around the track) if a 10K (6.2-mile) race is your goal and up to a mile if you are training for a marathon. The key ingredient in these workouts is to run slightly faster than your intended race pace.

Galloway's Book on Running suggests interval workouts of 5 to 7 seconds faster per lap than the 10K pace you plan to run in a race. Let's say your goal pace for an upcoming 10K race is 8 minutes per mile. On the track that equates to 2:00 per lap for four laps. Therefore, your goal for each repetition is 1:55 to 1:53 per lap (i.e., 5 to 7 seconds faster than a 2-minute lap). Six laps at that pace would be written as 6 × 440 @ 1:53. After each "speed" lap, jog a lap to rest or recover before continuing with the next speed lap. You can also decrease the length of your rest lap depending on your ability to recover.

Start this part of your training with four to six laps and increase by one or two each week. Interval workouts are generally begun about 8 to 10 weeks prior to the goal race. Ideally, several weeks of hill repeats should come before interval training in your running program. These workouts will help strengthen the propulsion muscles in your legs in preparation for the strain and intensity of interval workouts. Quality interval training improves your muscles' ability to use oxygen more efficiently. In addition, it teaches you how to run at an even pace. Knowing whether you are running too fast or too slow is an important skill at any distance.

TRY LADDER WORKOUTS

Ladder workouts are considered part of the interval family. The difference lies in the distance covered in each repetition. While repeat intervals prescribe running the same distance for each repetition, the distance is varied in laddering. Ladder workouts are therefore valuable for adding variety to your speed training and for providing a distance component as well.

"Ladders represent an efficient way to integrate speed training with specific endurance training," according to Brad Hudson in the book *Run Faster*. With ladder workouts, a runner completes a series of segments on the track arranged in order of ascending distance and decreasing pace (the longer the distance, the easier the pace) or decreasing distance and increasing pace (the shorter the distance, the faster the pace). Or a runner can do it both ways.

For example, the ladder can progress upward, starting with one lap of the track, then two, three, and four laps, with a recovery lap in between. The Olympian Frank Shorter is known to favor a downward ladder with sets of 1 × 1,600 meters, 1 × 1,200, 1 x 800, 2 × 400, and 4 × 200. One of Hudson's preferred ladder workouts in *Run Faster* consists of time-based segments arranged this way: a 6-minute run, followed by 5 minutes, then 4 minutes, 3 minutes, 2 minutes, and 1 minute, with a 1-minute recovery jog between each segment. The first segment is run at 10K-race pace. Each subsequent segment is run at a slightly faster pace than the one before it, with the last segment run at 1,500-meter or mile pace.

Ladder workouts done once every few weeks complement interval workouts by varying pace and distance. Therefore, they should be a component of any training program; we all need a change of pace once in a while.

Successful training results when
a runner puts all the pieces together.
Running is more than logging miles.
It's nutrition, strength, flexibility, recovery,
and everything else that gets a runner
to the finish line.

—Scott Jurek
Running coach and seven-time winner
of the Western States
100-Mile Endurance Run

ENTER A RACE

The difference between a jogger and a runner is an entry blank.

—*Dr. George Sheehan, writer and running philosopher*

According to Running USA, there were an estimated 10 million finishers in road races in 2009. The footrace is one of history's oldest sporting competitions, and the reasons for entering one are plentiful. The author and running coach Bob Glover says that "competitive running gives your running life focus." Some other reasons to enter a race:

- To measure your running fitness
- To gauge your improvement over time
- To experience a fast pace over a measured distance
- To feel a sense of accomplishment
- To be part of a social event with like-minded individuals
- To raise money for charity

Sprinkled throughout this book are examples of countless races: short ones, long ones, large ones, small ones, and those that are challenging, fun, risky, and weird and wacky. In each of these races there will be runners of all abilities: elite runners who are racing to win, and those who just want the satisfaction of finishing. Whatever your motivation, remember to have fun.

THE ONE RACE EVERYBODY SHOULD RUN

If you run only one race, make it this one. Nancy Brinker was inspired by her dying sister, Susan, who showed compassion for other breast cancer patients while she herself was dying of the disease. To fulfill a promise to her sister to do everything she could to find a cure for the disease, Nancy founded an organization and began the Susan G. Komen Race for the Cure. Each 5K (3.1-mile) run in the series raises funds and awareness for the fight against breast cancer, celebrates breast cancer survivorship, and honors those who have lost their battle with the disease. It is known as the most successful fund-raising and education event for breast cancer ever created, and recently celebrated its twenty-fifth anniversary.

The Race for the Cure takes place in more than a hundred cities across the country, from Albany to Aspen, Scranton to Sacramento. Visit www.komen.org to learn more about the organization, share your story, and search for the date and location of the race nearest you.

BEST RACE NAMES

Freeze Yer Gizzard Blizzard Run, International Falls, Minnesota

Long Haul in Your Long Johns Marathon, Indianola, Iowa

There's a Black Fly in My Eye 10-Mile Run, Gorham, New Hampshire

Cincinnati Flying Pig 1,0K, Cincinnati, Ohio

Run Like Hell 5K, Indianapolis, Indiana

Rumba on the Lumber, Lumberton, North Carolina

Dismal Swamp Stomp Half Marathon, Chesapeake, Virginia

The Jiggle Butt Run, Arlington, Texas

Franklin's Fat Ass 50K, Bozeman, Montana

Wascully Wabbit Twail Wun, Media, Pennsylvania

Low Country Hog Jog 5K, Hardeeville, South Carolina

Gaspin' in the Aspen Trail Run, Flagstaff, Arizona

Running with the Devil 50-Mile Run, Boulder City, Nevada

Tour de Pain 4-Mile, Jacksonville, Florida

Huffing for Stuffing Thanksgiving Day Run, Bozeman, Montana

Skirt Chaser 5K, Denver, Colorado

Will Run for Beer 5K, Newmarket, New Hampshire

Make It Hurt on the Dirt Duathlon, Butte, Montana

RUN THE ROCKY STEPS

It has one of the best art collections of any museum in the world, including works by Monet, Rembrandt, Cézanne, and other masters. A prized possession is one of the famous van Gogh "sunflower" paintings; another in that series previously sold for $40 million. But there are visitors to the Philadelphia Museum of Art who come not to admire the Monet landscapes, the Rembrandt portraits, or even the van Gogh sunflowers. No, they come for the steps.

Drive along the Benjamin Franklin Parkway past the Philadelphia Museum of Art on any day, and you'll see folks of all ages—alone or in groups—running up the museum steps and dancing joyfully with arms thrust in the air once they reach the top. Runners and nonrunners alike are simply reenacting one of the most famous scenes in movie history: when Sylvester Stallone in the movie *Rocky* sprints up the museum steps in gray sweats and high-top sneakers, confident that he is one lean, mean fighting machine and looking forward to the upcoming title fight. Yes, every runner should take inspiration from running the *Rocky* steps, as they are known locally.

Over the years, those steps have inspired not only runners but also marriage proposals and other nice deeds. The book *Rocky Stories: Tales of Love, Hope, and Happiness at America's Most Famous Steps,* relates various stories from people who made the pilgrimage from all corners of the United States to run in the footsteps of their movie hero. Be sure not to miss the controversial Rocky statue near the base of the steps but off to one side—"controversial" because the museum didn't care for the original location, which placed it atop those very steps, where it garnered more attention than the museum's renowned art collection. Years later a compromise brought it back to its current location.

More ambitious runners can do the *Rocky* steps as part of the 8.4-mile loop that hugs the Schuylkill River behind the museum. Afterward, whether you're an art lover or not, do take some time to go inside and pay your respects to the fabulous art collection, including that van Gogh. Just remember to take a shower first.

Find friends to run with.

—Greg Meyer
Past winner of the Boston
and Chicago Marathons

FIND A RUNNING PARTNER

Mark Twain once said that "to get the full value of a joy you must have somebody to divide it with." And what better joy to share than a run?

The perception of the loneliness of the long-distance runner derives from the image of that lone runner out on the roads in solitary training through rain, cold, early morning, and dark of night. Sure, most of your running may be done alone. Just you and the *slap-slap-slap* of your feet on the asphalt. On those solitary runs there is peace and time for inner reflection. But a running partner can lend encouragement and hold us accountable. He or she can help us over the final hill of a training run, share the pace during a 10K race, meet us at the local track for the weekly speed sessions, or get us out of bed for that Saturday-morning 18-miler. Indeed, according to running great Bill Rodgers, a training partner can be a key to your running and racing success.

A running partner is also a valuable source of feedback on your running form. With the ability to monitor your running mechanics from beside and behind you, a partner is more likely than you are to detect any chinks in that form before they become habitual. Likewise, since you and your running partner will eventually become familiar with each other's running style, a change in one's running form, however slight, may be easier to detect.

If you have no running buddies, look for one at your next race, at the fitness center, or at the local running club, or find another lone runner on a solitary run and strike up a conversation. You know there is at least one thing you both have in common.

LOVE ON THE RUN

If you and your running partner ever become more than just friends, the next step in your relationship might be a couples' race. Not surprisingly, many such races occur on or around Valentine's Day.

The Cal Poly Triathlon team of San Luis Obispo, California, sponsors the Chains of Love 5K/10K/15K Valentine's weekend, emphasizing a couples theme. People dressed as cupids serve as course marshals who lead the race, trail the last runner on the course, and give directions. Any lovers' quarrel that occurs along the course will most likely be forgotten at the finish, as all racing couples must cross the line holding hands. The race recently partnered with Pocket of Change, a charity that provides supplies and volunteers to an orphanage in Kenya. Ten percent of the race proceeds is donated to that charity, along with any extra race T-shirts. All entrants are encouraged to bring a gently used item of clothing to donate as well.

All kinds of couples, from husbands and wives, fathers and daughters, and those who want to get in a run and go on a date at the same time, can enter the Bradford Valentine Road Races, which have been held in Bradford, Massachusetts, since 1996. What makes this couples' race different from others is that one teammate must run the 6K (3.7-mile) race while the other runs the 5-mile race, for a combined time. Flowers and a box of chocolates are given to every finisher.

Not yet part of a couple? Maybe you can find that special someone at www.fitness-singles.com, a matchmaking site "if you're an athletic single in search of a fitness date to share your adventures and enthusiasm." If love does blossom on the road, on the trail, or on the track, the next stop could be the Las Vegas Marathon. There, couples can get married at the Run-Thru Wedding Chapel at mile 5, where they can profess their love (and their love of running) before 20,000 witnesses.

Paavo Nurmi

Paavo Nurmi is one of only four athletes to win nine Olympic gold medals and the only distance runner to do so. He dominated distance running in the 1920s and is the most decorated track-and-field athlete in Olympic history. Rather than performing well in one or two events, the "Flying Finn" excelled in the 1,500, 3k, 5k, 10k, steeplechase, and cross-country. Nurmi was one of the first athletes to realize the value of cross-training as well as pacing and was feared for his even but challenging pace throughout a race that few could match. "Others can't hold the pace," he said, "if it is steady and hard all through to the tape."

Always listen to your body, and don't be
afraid to take days off!

—Suzy Favor Hamilton
Three-time Olympian
in the 1,500-meters

LISTEN TO YOUR BODY

Maybe you've heard experts, such as the Olympian Suzy Favor Hamilton, advise runners to "listen to your body" when training, but you never had a clear idea what they meant. Consequently, you ignored clues that you were sick or overtraining and eventually suffered an illness or injury as a result. Your body provides you with constant feedback that can help improve your performance. Learning to interpret that feedback, whether it's positive or negative, will go a long way in preventing injury and keeping you healthy.

"Listening to your body" means learning to recognize all the different signals of pain and fatigue that may result from running too fast, too long, or too often. Of course, some minor pain and fatigue is expected as the body adjusts to increased training. And fighting through some discomfort and weariness in a race is necessary if you want to stay competitive. But doing so continually is asking for trouble.

Some indications that you may need to back off include:

- Pain in joints, muscles, or tendons that is more severe than usual
- Trouble falling asleep or staying asleep
- More colds, fever blisters, and runny noses
- Frequent irritability
- A general tiredness that lasts for days or weeks

Olympian Pete Pfitzinger writes on his training Web site www.pfitzinger.com that sometimes he forced his body to do more than it could handle. "The signals were always there in the form of pain or fatigue. The results of ignoring those signals have invariably been more time off from running than if I had paid attention and backed off training sooner."

GET ENOUGH REST

You are probably not getting as much of it as you should, even though rest is an essential part of any training program. When discussing training regimens in his book *The Complete Book of Running,* Jim Fixx wrote, "You're asking your body to do things it's never been called upon to do—at least not for a long time—and it responds by obligingly restructuring itself to make its various parts more efficient." That is, exercise stresses muscles and stimulates them to grow stronger. But in order for your body to make repairs and grow stronger, it needs adequate rest.

The running author and Olympian Jeff Galloway (one of this book's contributors) has coached more than one million runners through his running schools, retreats, e-coaching, books, and individual consultations. His books have low-mileage, proven plans to stay injury-free while training for significant goals such as marathons. Not surprisingly, Jeff believes the "R" word is the most important training principle. "Without enough rest after the stress," he says in *Marathon: You Can Do It!,* "the muscles are driven to exhaustion or injury. Stress must be balanced by rest in sufficient quantity and quality for adequate growth." Growth, in this case, refers to the positive physiological benefits of more and bigger mitochondria in the cells, an increase in oxygen-transporting capillaries, and stronger cell walls and blood vessels. The body needs days, not hours, to repair stress-related damage to the cells so they will be ready for the next workout. And with adequate rest, improved performance is much more likely.

Rest can come in the form of easy training days that follow hard days, easy training weeks that follow hard weeks, and days off with no running at all.

With all the miles ultra running superstar Scott Jurek puts in, you'd think he'd have little, if any, time to rest. Think again. As he writes on his blog at www.scottjurek.com, "I've always taken 4–6 weeks off at the end of every race season to let my muscles and mind mend from the long months of hard racing and training. I truly believe this recovery period has been instrumental in enabling me to churn out top race results year after year."

BON VOYAGE! A CRUISE FOR RUNNERS

You may have heard that cruises are for the newly wed, the overfed, or the nearly dead. Well, this one is different. "My wife always wanted to go on a cruise, and I never did. Being a runner and an active person, I thought people just ate, drank, and sat around on the ship." That's what race organizer Jerry Friesen thought about vacation cruises until he had a brainstorm. "One cold winter day when I was out running, I got to thinking about running in the Caribbean and if running off a cruise ship would be possible. Maybe I could organize an event."

That event and others eventually became part of the Cruise to Run vacation, now in its fourth year. Jerry and his wife, Jody, team up with Princess Cruises to take runners to popular Caribbean islands, where runs and races are organized under the supervision of local authorities. A sample itinerary: a 5K (3.1-mile) run on Saint Thomas; an 8-mile out-and-back run on Antigua; 5 miles to the lighthouse on St. Lucia; a 5K race on Barbados. The cruise package comes complete with runner's bibs, chip timing, trophies, and beautiful tropical beaches for swimming or sunbathing after each event.

Back on board, passengers can listen to guest speakers such as the well-known marathoner and author Dick Beardsley. A commendable activity to undertake on these trips is the Runners Give Back program. Runners can take a book onshore to donate to a local library, buy a race T-shirt to support the local running community, or donate a pair of running shoes to benefit a less fortunate athlete on one of the islands.

"The response has been overwhelming," says Friesen, with 303 runners and 45 guests taking the most recent voyage—more than twice the number of passengers who signed on for the inaugural cruise. "How can we go wrong when we have this many like-minded people doing what they love to do while on vacation?"

Not a beach person? Cruise to Run Alaska will soon set sail from Seattle. Visit www.cruisetorun .com for more information.

RUN UNDER A FULL MOON

If you've ever run by an open field at night and wondered why the moon looks big at the horizon and smaller when it's higher up, you're not alone. Even Aristotle was puzzled by the fact that the rising moon at the horizon looks considerably larger than it does later, at higher elevations. But that's beside the point. The point is that you were out running under a full moon, experiencing the serenity of running late at night with your path illuminated by the soft embrace only moonlight can provide.

If you look at the race calendar, it appears that many others ignore the warning in Creedence Clearwater Revival's "Bad Moon Rising" by specifically scheduling and entering races that are run under a full moon. There's the Mystic Runners Full Moon 5K (3.1 miles) in Wakefield, Massachusetts, the Sheboygan County Full Moon Half Marathon (13.1 miles) in Wisconsin, and the Harvest Moon Ten Miler in, appropriately, Moon Township, Pennsylvania.

Perhaps the most interesting in this category is the E.T. Full Moon Marathon, Half Marathon, and 10K in Rachel, Nevada. Competitors follow a point-to-point course through the Nevada desert on Highway 375, also known as the Extraterrestrial Highway. Runners may find some unlikely companions pacing them out there under the moonlight since the highway is rumored to have the most active extraterrestrial activity anywhere in the world.

Of course, full-moon runners or racers should always take the necessary precautions of reflective clothing and traffic awareness. They should also be prepared to find that Mother Nature is not always dependable, as organizers of the Full Moon 5K in Scottsdale, Arizona, note on their Web page: "We recommend and encourage you to run with a flashlight or headlamp as moonlight doesn't always cooperate with us."

Refueling within thirty minutes after a run
is key.

—Hazel Clark
Five-time U.S. 800-meter champion
Member of the 2008 Olympic team

FUELING BEFORE AND AFTER A RUN

Making vegetables, whole grains, and fruit the foundation of each meal will ensure that your body receives the required percentage of calories from carbohydrates. Carbohydrates are broken down and stored in the muscles as glycogen, the energy source that is converted to the fuel needed for running. Here are some basic rules of thumb on what to eat just before and just after a workout.

Before: Research has shown that performance improves when carbohydrates are consumed an hour before exercise. Try to aim for about 100 to 200 grams of carbohydrates at this time. Foods with a low glycemic index enhance endurance by providing the body with a slow, steady stream of fuel. Also be sure to be adequately hydrated.

After: Muscles are most receptive to having their glycogen supply replaced within the first 30 minutes after a workout. High-glycemic-index foods, such as bagels, rice cakes, and energy bars, which provide short bursts of energy, are more appropriate at this time. Consume at least 8 to 12 ounces of water or sports drink to help rehydrate.

In her *Food Guide for New Runners,* the nutritionist Nancy Clark suggests combining carbohydrates (to refill glycogen stores) with protein (to repair muscle damage) after a workout. Her choices include cereal with milk, turkey on a baguette, yogurt with fruit, or a nice glass of chocolate milk. She also says, off the record, that all runners should indulge themselves, at least once in their life, with a few thick slices of French toast with real maple syrup after a long run!

Experiment with the amount, type, and timing of your pre- and post-exercise fuel to ensure adequate energy without cramps, diarrhea, or other discomfort. Or, just follow the simple strategy of masters runner Alex Ratelle, as noted in *The Quotable Runner:* "I eat whatever the guy who beat me in the last race ate."

WATCH YOUR WATER INTAKE

During the Twin Cities Marathon and 10 Mile, runners will consume about 252,000 cups of water. Unfortunately, some may drink more than they should without realizing the consequences. We all know that runners are told to drink early and often to avoid dehydration, especially in longer races. But in recent years experts have been trying to get the word out that too much water can cause more harm than good. Excessive water intake during endurance sports can dilute the sodium levels in the body. Water levels rise, the cells begin to swell, and the swelling can lead to disorientation, nausea, and in rare cases, death. This imbalance of water to sodium is called hyponatremia.

In 2005, the *New England Journal of Medicine* published a study showing that excessive fluid consumption, as evidenced by substantial weight gain while running, is the single most important factor associated with this condition. The study also revealed that a finishing time of more than four hours also correlates with hyponatremia, suggesting that slower runners are especially at risk. Why? They actually need less water because they will not lose as much through perspiration, but they are on the course longer than the faster runners and therefore have more opportunities to drink at each water stop. Notably, results from the study were the same when sports drinks, rather than water, were consumed.

More recent guidance from the scientific community is for runners merely *to replace the fluid they're losing* in long races rather than to drink as much as possible at each water stop. To help, you can determine your "hourly sweat rate," or the amount of fluid you lose primarily through sweat during each hour you exercise. This will provide guidance for the amount of fluid you should consume each hour while exercising in order to stay well hydrated. You can estimate your sweat rate by weighing yourself before and after an hour-long run and using a formula like the one suggested by the American College of Sports Medicine (weight lost during exercise per hour + fluid consumed during exercise per hour = hourly sweat rate).

COOK-FREE FOODS WHEN YOU NEED TO EAT AND RUN

Here's a sampling of good, healthy food choices for runners when convenience is a priority.

Easiest sources of CALCIUM	Low-fat milk, yogurt, and cheese; calcium-fortified orange juice; soy milk; tofu
Convenient PROTEINS	Deli roast beef, ham, and turkey; tuna; canned salmon; hummus; peanut butter; tofu; cottage cheese
Cook-free GRAINS	High-fiber breakfast cereals, wholesome breads and bagels, whole grain crackers
Best FRUITS for vitamins A and/or C	Oranges, grapefruit, tangerines, bananas, cantaloupe, strawberries, kiwi
VEGETABLES for vitamins A and/or C	Broccoli, spinach, tomatoes, carrots, green and red peppers, sweet potatoes, winter squash

Source: Nancy Clark, *Food Guide for Marathoners.*

Remember that food is fuel (not "fattening") and that food is also more powerful than medicine. Not one drug is more powerful than food in terms of effectively preventing/combating heart disease, high blood pressure, diabetes, cancer, osteoporosis, and other diseases of aging. If good health is your wish, eat wisely and well!

—Nancy Clark
Internationally known
sports nutritionist and
nutrition author

RUN ON INDEPENDENCE DAY

In a letter to his wife, Abigail, concerning the adoption of the Declaration of Independence by Congress, John Adams wrote, "I am apt to believe that it will be celebrated by succeeding generations as the great anniversary festival . . . it ought to be solemnized with pomp and parade, with shows, games, sports, guns, bells, bonfires, and illuminations, from one end of this continent to the other, from this time forward forever more."

In all likelihood, one of the "sports" Adams was considering was a good old-fashioned footrace, which makes you wonder who among George Washington, Adams, and Thomas Jefferson would have been fastest in the first-ever Philly 5K? What better way to celebrate our independence than by entering a race on our nation's birthday?

Atlanta's Peachtree Road Race is the largest of the Independence Day races, with more than 50,000 runners. Unofficially, more races are run on the Fourth of July than on any other day of the year. And why not? We aren't celebrating just life, liberty, and the pursuit of happiness but also our freedom to run wherever, whenever, and however we please. And that includes the July Fourth Butt Prints 5K Run in Williamson, New York, which celebrates the freedom to run wearing nothing at all!

BY THE NUMBERS

35.9	Estimated runners (in millions) overall in the United States
7.8	Estimated U.S. runners (in millions) who run 110+ days a year
2,250	Portable toilets at the New York City Marathon
86	Flights of stairs racers climb in the Empire State Building Run-up
13	Runners needed to make a 60-foot-long "centipede" in the Bay to Breakers race
13.1	Miles in a half marathon
467,000	U.S. marathon finishers in 2009
0.6	Seconds by which Roger Bannister broke the four-minute mile
45	Years for which Britain's Ron Hill has not missed taking a daily run
4:44	Average per mile pace by Haile Gebrselassie during his world-record marathon
16.1	Miles per hour Hicham El Guerrouj averaged during his world-record mile
25	Number of laps in a 10-kilometer race on an Olympic-size track
14,400	Bananas distributed to competitors in the Los Angeles Marathon
35	Years for which Jim Ryun held the U.S. national high school mile record of 3:55.3 minutes
5	Times Bill Rodgers stopped on the course during his U.S.-record marathon
303	Calories burned in 20 minutes of running at 8 minutes per mile by a 160-pound runner
2,000	Pounds of chocolate distributed to competitors in the Comrades Marathon
64,000	Participants in the 2009 Stracittadina Fun Run in Rome, Italy

Joan Benoit Samuelson

Joan Benoit Samuelson was one of the pioneers of women's marathoning. She won two Boston Marathons, setting the world record at that distance in 1983, and the Chicago Marathon in 1985, with an American record that lasted 18 years. Perhaps her greatest achievement was winning the inaugural Olympic Marathon for women in 1984. Before then, no women's running event over 1,500 meters had been included in the Olympics. Fourteen minutes into that race, Joan made an aggressive surge that none of the other runners could match. She ran the rest of the race alone, winning by a comfortable 400-meter margin. What was also notable about her victory was that it was achieved just seventeen days after knee surgery. Competing recently as a masters runner, Samuelson set an American indoor record for women 50 and older in the 3,000-meter run at the age of 51.

TAKE A RUN IN THE RAIN

Some of us spend so much time trying to get in out of the rain that we seldom think about actually going out and running *in* the rain. If you have never done it, take a nice leisurely run in the rain and see why so many others enjoy it.

The running author Jim Fixx was one of those people. "One day I was running and it began to pour," he wrote in *The Complete Book of Running.* "It was a warm day, and even though I was quickly soaked, I was happy and comfortable." Some runners enthuse about the calming effect a steady rain has on their psyche. Others claim that a run seems less strenuous in a cooling drizzle, no matter how fast the pace. And some look forward to how that rain freshens the air they are inhaling and exhaling.

If rainy weather has ever caused you to put off more than a few scheduled runs, that's even more reason to finally go out and have fun in the rain like you did as a kid. If you're still not sold on the idea, just remember that not every race you enter will be run in the warm sunshine and you may wish you had more experience running in the wet stuff, at least for the mental preparation.

A hat with a brim is a must if you decide to take the plunge. A wicking layer against the body and a wind- and water-resistant outer layer should be enough to keep the rest of you warm and dry. And remember: no pain, no gain—no rain, no rainbow.

REVISIT STRETCHING

If you're like most runners, you don't stretch nearly enough. But maybe that's a good thing. The purpose of stretching is to improve flexibility and minimize the chance of injury. Recent research, however, suggests that there is no clear evidence that it does either. Furthermore, stretching with bad form or with tight muscles is actually one of the leading causes of injury in runners.

Many detractors point to an official government review of previous studies on the benefits of stretching. The review was conducted by the Centers for Disease Control and Prevention and published in the March 2004 issue of the journal *Medicine & Science in Sports & Exercise.* The conclusion? "There is not sufficient evidence to endorse or discontinue routine stretching before or after exercise to prevent injury among competitive or recreational athletes. Further research . . . is urgently needed to determine the proper role of stretching in sports." In other words, the jury is still out.

It does appear, however, that a good warm-up can help. Evidence in the review suggests that if one starts by moving through a range of motions that will be used during the activity, such as walking or jogging for a runner, one is less likely to be injured. Therefore, slowly exercising the muscles before the activity instead of stretching them is advised.

Still, many people say stretching should still be a component of any fitness program as a form of preventive maintenance. Stretching in the evenings or throughout the day when the body is warmed up and relaxed is a good alternative to stretching right before the activity. Try for a regular routine several times a week, and concentrate at first on the key muscle groups that are tightened during running: calf muscles and Achilles tendons; hamstrings; and the lower back. Many books and videos are available that show how to *gently* and *correctly* stretch these muscle groups.

RACE AS A TEAM

Let's face it, even in the sea of humanity of a big race, it can get pretty lonely out there. Many times it's just you against the clock, with no one to encourage or push you and no one waiting at the finish to see how you did. For something different, run a team race. Not only will you have others on your side, they'll be counting on you as well.

The classic team-oriented races are the corporate challenges, in which teams of office colleagues compete against other teams in the name of fitness and corporate camaraderie. Typically, the team with the fastest collective time wins. The granddaddy of them all is the JPMorgan Chase & Co. Corporate Challenge (www.jpmorganchasecc.com), having been contested for more than thirty years. Among the current U.S. and international cities in this series are New York, Buffalo, Boston, Chicago, San Francisco, Sydney, Johannesburg, London, and Frankfurt. In 2009, the JPMorgan races exceeded 221,000 participants from more than 7,700 companies. The 3.5-mile distance for each race in the series was selected on the theory that it was "a distance for which even a busy executive would have time to train." Tell *that* to your overweight, workaholic boss!

Perhaps the most interesting, and certainly challenging, team concept is the Centipede division of San Francisco's Bay to Breakers 12K (7.4 miles). Each 60-foot-long "centipede" consists of thirteen runners plus one floater who runs alongside, substituting for runners who lose a shoe, drop off the pace, or need to make a pit stop. "Feelers" must be worn on the head of each centipede segment, while the final segment must wear a "stinger." A team must finish the race with 13 runners, including at least 12 of the original runners composing the centipede plus the floater, in order to be considered official.

For another exciting team running event . . .

RUN A RELAY

In relays, runners take the team concept to another level by running one or more individual segments, which contribute to the team's overall time for the race. These races are available in many distances, so the length and number of individual legs a team member is required to run vary by event. For example, a 10K (6.2-mile) relay would have two teammates run 3.1 miles each. A marathon relay typically has four runners completing legs of approximately 6 to 7 miles each. And a triathlon relay will have a swimmer, a cyclist, and a runner doing separate legs. Some of the most fun can be had in ultra distance relays, which require larger teams, with each teammate running multiple legs.

The first Hood to Coast Relay in 1982 consisted of 8 teams of 10 runners each. Now, with 1,000 teams, 12,000 runners, and 3,500 volunteers, the race is the largest relay in the world. How popular is it? For eleven straight years registration for all 1,000 teams has closed after just one day. The course begins at Timberline Lodge (elevation 6,000 feet) on Oregon's Mount Hood and ends 197 miles later at the Pacific Ocean in the coastal town of Seaside. Each leg ranges in distance from 3.7 to 7.4 miles. Not surprisingly, the first leg is a severe downhill covering 2,000 vertical feet over 5.6 miles. As in other large relays, the teams are self-supporting, meaning they are responsible for acquiring their own support vans able to hold upward of 12 sweaty runners and stocking them with their own water, food, first-aid supplies, and, most important, deodorant. In 2009, this "mother of all relays" helped raise $360,000 for the American Cancer Society. Visit its Web site at www.hoodtocoast.com for more information.

"Get your ass over the pass!" is the motto of Colorado's Wild West Relay. This 24-hour relay from Fort Collins to Steamboat Springs begins in the foothills of the Rocky Mountains and ends in the famous ski resort after crossing the Continental Divide. Teams visit Roosevelt, Medicine Bow, and Routt National Forests, and several small mountain and ranching communities along the route. By the time they reach the finish, they will have climbed over 16,000 cumulative feet of elevation. At 200 miles and 36 legs, the race requires each runner in a 12-person team to run three legs. For example, runner number 1 on each team will complete legs 1, 13, and 25, with each leg averaging about 5.25 miles. For individual runners looking to join a team, or for a team looking for runners, the race's Web site, www .wildwestrelay.com, has a Team Matching message board.

Because of the remoteness of the Wild West Relay course, volunteers are essential to act as race marshals and aid workers at middle-of-nowhere aid stations. Therefore, all teams are required to supply three nonracing volunteers to the relay. An innovative volunteer program first used by this race is called Volunteers with a Purpose. Instead of supplying their own volunteers, teams may choose to make a 100 percent tax-deductible donation to this organization. The donations are given in exchange for the groups' volunteer efforts at the relay. The entire amount donated is then distributed to local nonprofit groups in areas through which the relay is run.

RUN BACKWARD

The list of world record holders in the mile includes some of the most famous names in all of track: Roger Bannister, Herb Elliot, Jim Ryun, Sebastian Coe, and Hicham El Guerrouj. Then there's Thomas Dold. If his name is not as familiar as the others, it's because he didn't accomplish his mile record the way the rest did; he did it *backward*. Backward running, running backward, or simply "retro running" is taking Europe by storm as a healthy alternative to running the old-fashioned way. All "regular" runners should consider adding a little retro running to their weekly routine.

If you've ever snickered at someone running backward at the local track, well, no one laughed when Xu Zhenjun of China did it for 26.2 miles in the brisk time of 3 hours and 43 minutes. Indeed, the Chinese are considered the pioneers of running backward, having practiced the sport for thousands of years, according to www.backward-running-backward.com. Those behind this Web site are pushing for a backward-run marathon in the 2012 Olympics. And why not? Backward runners have already competed in the 2006, 2008, and 2010 Retro Running World Championships.

Proponents of retro running say it causes less trauma to the body since the runner is striking the ground on the toes rather than with the heel-toe combination of forward running. Furthermore, backward running is done at a much slower pace, which reportedly reduces the occurrence of muscle pulls and tears. In the book *Backwards Running*, Robert K. Stevenson asserts that this method builds stamina, restores good posture, promotes balance, adds variety, improves quickness, and strengthens leg muscles. In terms of that last benefit, Stevenson argues that forward running overdevelops the hamstring muscles at the expense of weakening the quadriceps. So, instead of an ideal 60/40 quad/hamstring strength ratio, many distance runners have a 50/50 or even a 40/60 ratio. "Backwards running," he writes, "is one of the few natural ways to bring about in your leg a balanced 60/40 quad/hamstring strength ratio."

Always go over a road race course or
a cross-country course ahead of time
and figure out the tangents and
the shortest possible line that you can
run the race and still be legal.

—Craig Virgin
Two-time world
cross-country champion
Three-time Olympian

RUNNING THE TANGENTS

If you were given the opportunity to run in the same race as any other runner but for a shorter distance, would you do it? What if it was completely legal?

It's called "running the tangents" and follows the principle we learned in geometry class that the shortest distance between two points is a straight line. A tangent, by definition, is a straight line that touches a curve. Certified road race courses are measured following the tangents rather than by following the winding path a car would take in the traffic lane. Therefore, if you run the tangents, you are running the actual measured race distance rather than the normal (and longer) course of the road.

In the diagram below of a curvy race course adapted from a design on runninginjuryfree.org, a runner follows the tangent by running a straight line from one curve to the next. In a course with many miles and many curves or turns, the distance saved by running the tangents can be significant.

The key to running the tangents in a race is to keep alert to the nature of the course and look ahead to plot the straightest line through the curves. Also, be aware of other runners close to you so as not to impede them as you navigate from one side of the road to the other to stay on line. Of course, this tactic should be used only in racing, not during regular runs, for as we all know, there are no shortcuts in training!

THE MOST FUN RACES

What can be fun about running 13.1 miles? Plenty if it's part of the Rock 'n' Roll race series. Take the Rock 'n' Roll in Virginia Beach Marathon in Virginia Beach, Virginia, for example. Runners begin at the Virginia Beach Convention Center and navigate the scenic oceanfront course that ends along the boardwalk. With fourteen different bandstands and sixteen local high school cheerleading squads, there are music and spirit from start to finish along the route. No surprise, then, that the race made the list of *Runner's World*'s "Better Halfs." The Rock 'n' Roll Marathon and Half Marathon series has other "tour" dates in Seattle, Chicago, San Diego, San Jose, Las Vegas, and Scottsdale, Arizona.

The Muddy Buddy 10K (6.2-mile) race series requires team members to alternate trail running with mountain biking while overcoming five challenging-but-fun obstacles. At the first obstacle, the rider drops the bike, completes the obstacle, and begins running. Then the running teammate arrives, completes the same obstacle, finds the bike, and begins riding. Teams continue leapfrogging each other through the entire course, facing such obstacles as a wall, a cargo net crawl, and a balance beam. At the end of the race, both racers must get down and dirty to conquer the infamous Mud Pit before crossing the finish line together. Muddy Buddy races are held in thirteen cities across the country.

Participants in San Francisco's Bay to Breakers 12K (7.4 miles) enjoy fun and folly in a carnival-like atmosphere while crossing the city from the Embarcadero to the Pacific Ocean. The event began in 1912 as the Cross City Race, with fewer than 200 entrants. Now this quintessential San Francisco event has swelled to nearly 70,000 participants, accompanied by live music and 100,000 spectators. The B2B, as the locals call it, originated the concept of costumed runners, according to the organizers. Each year, thousands run in the highly competitive costume division that bestows awards in the categories of Most Creative, Best Current Event, Best California-themed, and Best Green-themed. With so much fun going on, it's no surprise that a significant number of participants come back year after year in this celebration of the human spirit, including a blind runner who has competed in 42 consecutive races.

The Race to Robie Creek half marathon of Boise, Idaho, comes with a steadily climbing rise in elevation for the first eight miles, then switches to dirt roads as the course winds through the mountains. After that the route turns downhill, with a nasty hairpin turn at mile 9. So where's all the fun? At the start and the finish, that's where. Over the years, race organizers have found unique and entertaining ways to start each race, which are always a closely guarded secret. Starts have featured an exploding feather-filled balloon, a 300-pound Samoan jumping on a flip board to launch a coconut, a parachutist, Jell-O-filled papier-mâché toads dropped from a high platform, and a wedding, with the intent for runners to start the demanding race with smiles on their faces. While the Race to Robie Creek is meant to be fun, entry fees and contributions from local businesses benefit several area charities.

Another type of race seemed like a lot of fun to the twelve junk-food junkies who first devised the event in 2004. They would start from the bell tower on the North Carolina State University campus and run two miles to the Krispy Kreme store in downtown Raleigh. There, they would consume a dozen of the famous Krispy Kreme glazed doughnuts before running the two miles back to campus—all within one hour! Now that the word is out, entrants in the annual Krispy Kreme Challenge have been numbering in the thousands. There is no penalty for getting sick along the course, although "the real challenge is to keep all 12 down," according to race organizers. The event raises thousands of dollars each year to benefit North Carolina Children's Hospital.

The Web site of the Reno-Tahoe Odyssey stipulates that "everyone must have fun." Indeed, race director Eric Lerude says, "Most runners are in this event for the experience, not competitive running." The 178-mile, 12-person team relay traverses the alpine forests and snowcapped peaks of the Sierras and the northern Nevada high desert, where sightings of bears, coyotes, and wild mustangs are common. Competitors will also run through ghost towns, along part of the original Pony Express route, and beside beautiful Lake Tahoe. Prizes are awarded for the Most Spirited Team, the Best Custommade Team Shirts, the Best Decorated Team Vehicles, and the Best Team name. Recent entrants have included the Tahoe Trail Babes, the Heavy Breathers, the Mixed Bag of Nuts, Bear Bait, and Sisters and Misters with Blisters. A friendly competition among race volunteers for the Most Spirited Exchange Point ensures that race volunteers get in on the fun too.

RUNNING WITH ROVER

Dogs are great running companions. They provide a sense of security, never criticize your running form, adjust to whatever pace you select, require very little training, are almost always willing to run, and don't bore you with the details of their latest race. Indeed, running with your dog is an excellent way to keep up with your training while spending time with one of your best companions. Not only that, but your dog will also benefit from the additional exercise. No dog? No problem. Maybe you know an elderly neighbor whose dog could use some fresh air and exercise or some other friendly pooch that is bouncing off the walls just waiting for the chance to run with somebody.

Don't look now, but dog running is quickly becoming a competitive sport—for dogs *and* people. Dog Run Dog sponsors a 5K (3.1-mile) and 10K (6.2-mile) national racing circuit for teams of two- and four-legged runners. Currently these races are held in 10 cities throughout the country; about 20 more cities have expressed interest in holding future events. To qualify to run in these races, dogs must be at least one year old; otherwise they must be walked or carried. Be mindful too that each team is responsible for, well, scooping!

Whether racing or just running with Rover, www.dogrundog.com offers tips on how to run with man's best friend. These include:

- Start by taking your dog for long walks of at least half a mile every other day. After a week or so, sprinkle periods of running during the walks. Keep decreasing the walking over a week or two until your routine is all running.
- Gradually add speed and distance, but no more than a 10 percent increase in distance each week. If your dog starts lagging, slow down.
- For every day you run, give Rover a day off.

- Take your dog running on a soft surface, like grass and dirt trails. Concrete, hot asphalt, frozen roads, ice, and salt can all be harmful to the paws.
- Realize that dogs do not dissipate heat as efficiently as humans do. Rather than sweating, they lose heat through their paws and mouths. Plan your running route to allow drinking stops. Let the dog run through puddles and sprinklers.
- After the run, first offer sips of water for cooling down, rather than free access to water.
- Most important, make running fun for the dog. Talk to your dog and offer praise along the route.

Make a habit of running strides after
at least two of your weekly runs. Strides
are generally short bursts of up-tempo
running, usually between fifty and
one hundred meters, at a pace faster
than your current 5K race pace. Jog
an equal distance between each "stride"
for a recovery. Strides help to keep
specific muscle groups in tone and
promote balanced muscle groups.
Think of strides as "push-ups" for
your legs. I try to run one stride for
every mile I run that day.

—Keith Brantly
1996 Olympic marathoner
1998 U.S. marathon champion

CROSS-TRAIN

There are three main reasons all runners should include cross-training in their overall fitness program: it enhances aerobic fitness; it provides alternative exercises to do when injured; and it adds variety to prevent muscle imbalance and boredom.

When deciding on various cross-training methods, it's best to choose workouts that are closest to running in terms of the aerobic effort that will be expended, such as those shown on the next page. For injured runners, cross-training provides an alternative to just sitting on the sidelines, since most running injuries still allow you to do other aerobic activities. The road to recovery begins, however, only if the cross-training minimizes the trauma to the body caused by all that pavement pounding.

The alternative forms of exercise in cross-training regimens also helps minimize muscle imbalance. Sure, running strengthens the propulsion muscles (i.e., hamstrings, buttocks, and calf muscles), but it does little to strengthen other muscle groups. You can add cycling, therefore, to work the quads and swimming to work the upper body, while still receiving a great aerobic workout. Finally, if you ever feel your regular running routine getting a bit stale, cross-training will give you a needed break. The alternative exercises will keep your fitness level high, add variety to your training, and keep your overall running program fresh.

Maybe you're thinking that all these alternative exercises will prevent you from keeping up with your weekly mileage. If so, be sure to read the sections "Get Enough Rest," "Avoid Burnout," and "Listen to Your Body." You may also want to pay attention to Ed Eyestone. The former Olympian and cross-training advocate writes in *Runner's World* that runners can actually boost their weekly mileage with cross-training. He asserts that an hour of intense cross-training can deliver the equivalent aerobic benefits of a 5-mile training run. Following that simple formula, a week with 25 miles of running and 5 hours of cross-training will bring your total "mileage" for the week to 50. Feel better now?

BEST CROSS-TRAINING WORKOUTS FOR RUNNERS

"Running helps me stay on an even keel and in an optimistic frame of mind."
—Bill Clinton

"Out on the roads there is fitness and self-discovery and the persons we were destined to be."
—Dr. George Sheehan

"Wisely, and slow. They stumble that run fast."
—William Shakespeare, *Romeo and Juliet*

"I want to run until I can't run."
—Bill Rodgers

"Don't run as hard as you can. Run as fast as you can without straining."
—Jack Daniels

FIND YOUR INNER BILLY MILLS

The race was expected to be between world record holder Ron Clarke of Australia and Tunisia's Mohammed Gammoudi; all other runners would fight it out for the bronze medal. No one gave American Billy Mills a shot in that 1964 Olympic 10,000-meter run; few, if any, even knew who he was. And just as the experts predicted, the final meters came down to a battle between Clarke and Gammoudi—for *second* place.

In one of the greatest upsets in Olympic history, Billy Mills won the gold medal with a stunning come-from-behind finish after digging deep and finding a burst of energy in the final 25 meters. Sure, he had trained hard for that race, but, more important, he needed to keep believing in himself when no one else would, just as he had as an orphan growing up in poverty on an Indian reservation.

While his visualization training allowed him to believe he could run with the best in the world, he couldn't let his confidence be shattered when he qualified a minute slower than the favorite in the preliminaries. Nor could he stop believing when, during the final lap, he was bumped off stride and stumbled, losing valuable seconds. "At that point I was going to accept third place," he says on the must-see video of the race at www.flotrack.org/videos/play/142054-billy-mills-interview. But then, as he came around the final turn, still behind the leaders, his thoughts changed from "I can try . . . I can try," to "I can win! . . . I can win! . . . I can win!"

Mills's win, in which he ran an astounding 50 seconds faster than his previous best, was voted the Associated Press "Upset of the Year." But if you truly believe you can accomplish your goals—in a race, on a tough training run, or in life—a great performance is really not such an upset after all.

Go into any good running store, and you will see a poster of Billy Mills winning his Olympic race. Underneath is the quote "Every passion has its destiny." What will yours be?

WIN IN YOUR AGE GROUP

Most races have more than one winner, since awards are presented to the top male and female finishers in each of several age-group categories. If you are not able to finish first overall in a race, aim to win your age group.

To many, this is a fairer and more legitimate win anyway because it's more like comparing apples to apples. It's not the 44-year-old, 20-mile-a-week runner competing directly against the hotshot high school athlete. Rather, it's that 44-year-old competing against others in their forties. Sure, another runner in your age group can win the race overall, but age-group awards are organized in your favor. How? Most races do not recognize award duplication. Therefore, the overall winner, who might be age 27, can win only the first-place trophy, while *someone else* will win the award for being first in the 21-to-30 age group.

Obviously, if you want to increase your odds, you should aim for a race with a broad range of age-award categories. Many races will give awards to the top finishers ages 15 to 19, 20 to 24, 25 to 29, 30 to 34, and so on, rather than decade-specific awards for those in their twenties, thirties, forties, etc. Based on the size of the field, many races give awards to the top *three* in each category.

Listen to Hazel Clark if you need extra motivation to snag an age group award. "I recommend all runners run with abandon once in their lifetime," says the 2008 Olympian. "Maybe run a race that on paper seems unrealistic. You never want to wonder if there was more in the tank."

Theoretically, there is an advantage for someone at the lower end of the age category to win that age group. Indeed, masters runner Frank Levine set the American record in the 400-meter dash for men ages 95 to 99 soon after graduating into that age bracket. As he told *The New York Times,* "It makes you look forward to getting older."

YOU CAN FINISH LAST AND STILL WIN THIS RACE

Paavo Nurmi of Finland won more gold medals than any other distance runner in Olympic history partly because he knew the value of pacing. His strategy was to keep an even tempo throughout a race, often running with a stopwatch to ensure he wasn't going too fast or too slow. Eighty years since the "Flying Finn" won his last medal, a new race has emerged that stresses the importance of knowing your pace. What is compelling about this type of race is that it gives everyone an equal chance of winning, no matter how fast (or slow) they run and regardless of age or gender.

Such a race is called a prediction race. The winner is not necessarily the first runner across the finish line but the one whose actual finishing time comes closest to his or her predicted finishing time. For obvious reasons, there are no timers along the course, and runner's watches are a no-no.

Cedar Rapids, Iowa, promotes its Mall to Mall prediction race by noting "You don't have to be the fastest to win." Other such races include the Frostbite Prediction 5K in Cuyahoga Falls, Ohio, and the Fox River Fox and Turkey Prediction 4-Miler in Batavia, Illinois. According to the results from a past Fox and Turkey Prediction 4-Miler, the winner's predicted time was right on the ball, even though it was 4½ minutes *slower* than that of the runner-up.

FOR WOMEN RUNNERS ONLY

Girls Just Wanna Have Fun 5K, College Park, Maryland

Women Can Run 5K, Conway, Arkansas

Susan B. Anthony Women's 5K, Sacramento, California

She Rocks! Triathlon/Duathlon, Waterloo, Michigan

Alaska Run for Women 5-Miler, Anchorage, Alaska

See Jane Run Half Marathon, Alameda, California

Iron Girl Duathlon, Bloomington, Minnesota

Red Dress Run for Women 5K, Hartford, Connecticut

What Women Want Trail Run, Great Falls, Montana

Girls Inc. of New Hampshire 5K, Rochester, New Hampshire

Freihofer's Run for Women 5K, Albany, New York

MORE Marathon and Half-Marathon, New York, New York

Girls on the Run 5K, various locations nationwide

RUN THANKSGIVING MORNING

Thanksgiving is a time to be with loved ones and to recall all that you have to be thankful for during the year: family, friends, good health, prosperity, and running—though not necessarily in that order.

The main benefit of running Thanksgiving morning is that by piling on the miles, you can later pack in the calories without the slightest bit of guilt. Indeed, with that 10K you ran at 9 a.m., you don't have to think twice about having seconds on herbed stuffing, savory turkey, mashed potatoes, Granny's pumpkin pie, or that Jell-O dessert with the marshmallows on top.

Many will find a leisurely run in the brisk autumn air the perfect way to start their Thanksgiving Day. For those who like a little camaraderie and competition, there are countless Turkey Trots to enter. The Capital One Bank Dallas YMCA Turkey Trot, for example, calls itself the largest Thanksgiving Day event of its kind in the country. The 8-mile race began 40 years ago and now extends through generations of participants.

And for those who *really* expect to eat their fill later in the day, the Long Beach Turkey Trot allows runners to compete in *all three* of its races if they so desire. One can do the 5K (3.1 miles) at 7:30, the 10K (6.2 miles) at 8:30, and then stumble through another 5K at 9:30, all at no extra charge.

Yes, every runner should take a run Thanksgiving morning. It's an expression of appreciation for another good year of running and a way to make room for all the bounty at the Thanksgiving table—like that green bean casserole made with cream of mushroom soup and covered with burnt onions. Well, maybe there are some things we're not all that thankful for.

Don't time every training run. You're not always going to get faster, and the point is to do the distance.

—Don Kardong
Senior writer for *Runner's World*
1976 Olympic marathoner

AVOID DOG BITES

Dogs bite out of fear, to protect their territory, or to establish their dominance over the person being bitten. The Centers for Disease Control and Prevention estimates that about 4.5 million people are bitten by dogs each year, with about one in five victims requiring medical attention. Runners are particularly at risk since they inadvertently encroach on a dog's territory, arrive swiftly and without warning, and leave in a way that can excite a predator-versus-prey response from the offending pooch. Therefore, it behooves all runners to learn correct behavior around potentially hostile dogs when an encounter is unavoidable.

Taking a detour around dogs in open yards, unleashed dogs being walked by their owners, and away from the sound of barking dogs in the distance should be standard procedure. But a runner is often just as surprised as the dog when meeting one freely wandering the street or encountering one around the blind bend of a trail. Many groups, such as the Humane Society, provide tips on what to do when a dog/runner encounter cannot be avoided:

- Make noise to announce your presence to avoid catching the dog completely by surprise.
- Do not look the dog in the eye, as the dog may perceive this as a challenge.
- When you first come near a dog, let the animal see and sniff you. Any movement toward a dog should be from the side, not from the back or directly from the front.
- If an unfamiliar dog approaches, remain as still as possible with your arms at your sides. If the dog loses interest, move away slowly so as not to revive his interest.
- Do not run from a dog or scream. If a dog knocks you to the ground, curl into a ball and protect your face and head. Try to remain as motionless as possible until the dog goes away.
- If a bite occurs, wash the wound thoroughly with soap and water and apply an antiseptic. Contact a physician and report the dog to the local animal control agency.

Jim Ryun

In 1964, Jim Ryun became the first high school runner ever to break 4 minutes for the mile. Later, in 1966 at the age of 19, he set the mile world record, which was not broken until 1975. The former Sullivan Award winner, *Sports Illustrated* Sportsman of the Year, and ESPN "Best High School Athlete Ever" was a three-time Olympian in the 1,500, winning the silver medal in the 1968 Games. After coming out of retirement, Ryun was a favorite for the gold medal in the 1972 Olympics, but his hopes died when he fell 500 meters from the finish of his qualifying race. Though video evidence shows he was fouled, the Olympic Committee refused to reinstate him. From 1996 to 2007, Ryun served as the congressman for the 2nd Congressional District of Kansas. Many on Capitol Hill, however, never realized they were working alongside the last U.S. runner to hold the world record in the mile.

RUN NEW YEAR'S EVE

While nonrunners are getting drunk and watching the ball drop on TV, you can be away from all that, knowing full well that there's no better way to ring out the old and ring in the new than with a run.

Perhaps you'll feel a twinge of nostalgia on that run as you recall with satisfaction the number of miles logged the previous year, the confidence gained from the workouts you suffered through, and the fulfillment derived from your performance in the races you entered. Nostalgia will then be replaced with the anticipation of doing more of it in the New Year. There won't be any time for nostalgia, however, if you're competing in one of the many New Year's Eve races that have sprung up all over the country. Most likely, one of them is not far from you.

Perhaps the best known is the 4-mile Midnight Run in Central Park, sponsored by New York Road Runners, complete with costume parade and fireworks. Another is the Sacramento Fleet Feet Sports New Year's Eve Run, which begins along the city's Front Street Promenade. The 2-mile course steers runners to Old Sacramento for the New Year's festivities afterward. Or you can visit North Carolina's Outer Banks for the New Year's Eve 5K (3.1 miles) in Nags Head. It began one cold New Year's Eve with four brave runners and is now in its nineteenth year. Don't worry if you're a late arrival and forget your cash; the race is free and requires no registration. Happy New Year!

RUN NEW YEAR'S DAY

But if you can't stay up past midnight as in years past, greet the New Year with a run after a good night's sleep. And if you had a little too much to drink the night before, a run on the first day of the year is sure to clear your head. Just ask Mark Coogan. The 1996 Olympic marathoner counts a New Year's Day run as something every runner should do to jump-start the coming year and adds that it's also a good way to relieve a hangover.

To that end, the Hangover 5K (3.1 miles) of Salisbury Beach, Massachusetts, may be just the remedy. If the race doesn't help your hangover, maybe a dip in the Atlantic will; runners have the option of finishing their race with "The World Famous Beach Plunge." Just be aware that runners need to be *fully submerged* in the bone-chilling ocean to receive the coveted plunge mug.

The New Year's Day Hair of the Dog 5K in Virginia Beach, Virginia, lets you ring in the New Year in two optional race divisions. The formal wear division bestows awards on the top male and female runners who compete in their formal wear from the night before. In the Weight Division, runners can have their performance calculated based not on elapsed time but on seconds per pound.

Anyone can begin their resolution to run more often in the New Year by entering the 5K Resolution Run in Raleigh, North Carolina. Runners there can also win prizes for taking part in a prediction-run format by coming closest to the finishing time they predicted before the race. Mini–Resolution Runs are offered for those 6 years and under (100-meter race) and ages 6 to 10 (1/4 mile), and parents are encouraged to run with their children.

Speaking of resolutions, why not resolve to . . .

RUN EVERY DAY FOR AN ENTIRE YEAR

The United States Running Streak Association lists more than 40 members who have been running daily for 30 years or more. At the top of the list is Mark Covert, a teacher from California who hasn't missed a day since he was 17. He is now 59. England's Ron Hill is generally considered to have the world's longest streak, having run every day for the past 45 years.

According to the USRSA, a running streak is defined as "running at least one continuous mile within each calendar day under one's own body power." This can occur on the roads, a track, over hill and dale, or even on a treadmill. Running cannot occur using canes, crutches, or banisters, or in a pool. Some began their streaks for the health benefits of losing weight or keeping cholesterol and blood pressure under control. Others "streak" for the sense of order it bestows on their hectic lives. And some just love the *slap, slap, slap* poetry of one foot in front of the other—day after day after day.

Every experienced runner should give consideration to running every day for a full year—then, taking a break. Otherwise, you could find yourself years into a Cal Ripken–like streak you may have trouble ending. Consider the runner who kept his streak alive by jogging in a plaster cast after a bunion operation. Or the "streaker" (not to be confused with the naked variety) who ran several days with severe chest pains before realizing it was a heart attack rather than indigestion. Even Mark Covert admits that he once ran on a broken foot. Alas, the USRSA's official newsletter typically includes an article lamenting the end of a streak that had become an integral part of a runner's life, such as "Breaking Up (a Running Streak) Is Hard to Do," "Thanks for the Memories," and "Ding Dong, the Streak Is Dead."

Your running streak, whether active or retired, entitles you to USRSA membership. Once your streak reaches a year in duration, you qualify for a permanent USRSA listing. No doubt such a streak will be cherished as much as that dusty running trophy you have on the bookcase and will be an accomplishment you can happily share with your friends and grandkids, as well as your podiatrist.

YOUR COMPETITIVE CATEGORY

Bob Glover has more than 30 years of experience coaching runners. In *The Competitive Runner's Handbook,* he and his wife, Shelly-Lynn Florence Glover, an exercise physiologist, divide runners into several competitive categories in terms of performance. Of course, a runner may qualify for one category in one race distance and another category in a different distance. Which category fits you best?

Category	Interpretation
Novice/intermediate	Casual competitors or those new to competition. Their times will be slower than those of basic competitors.
Basic competitor	Typical "middle-of-the-pack" runners who have trained diligently and wisely. Over time, these runners may be able to move up to the next category.
Competitor	Runners at this level usually finish in the top one-third of the field and may place in some local races. This is the highest level of competition most runners can achieve due to limited ability or lack of time or discipline.
Advanced competitor	These runners have a fair amount of talent and/or a strong work ethic. Usually place in the top 10% to 25% of the field and may win awards in local events. Moving up to the next category requires a serious commitment and a strong talent base.
Local champion	Those able to reach the top local level due to talent, dedication, and energy. A category requiring serious competitive training. Can usually finish in the top 5 or 10 of his or her age group in local races and will sometimes win.
Semi-elite	Often win smaller races and place high in big ones.
Elite	The cream of the crop that run off with the big prize money in top races around the world.

PART III GET THE GEAR

GOOD BOOKS ON RUNNING AND TRAINING

Galloway's Book on Running preaches high performance along with pain-free running and has sold more than 400,000 copies since it was first published in 1984. A former Olympian who now coaches runners at clinics and retreats, Jeff Galloway provides a factual, easy-to-read book based on his personal experience working with more than 100,000 runners of all abilities. In addition to covering the essentials, such as starting out, racing, injuries, and food, the book includes week-by-week training programs for 5K (3.1-mile), 10K (6.2-mile), and half marathon (13.1-mile) races that emphasize more rest, less weekly mileage, and long runs every other week.

"Everything You Need to Know to Run for Fun, Fitness and Competition" is the subtitle of *Runner's World Complete Book of Running*. *Runner's World* magazine executive editor and former Boston Marathon winner Amby Burfoot has gathered advice from well-known running authors such as Joe Henderson, Hal Higdon, and Jerry Lynch, as well as nutrition editor Liz Applegate, and presented it in an attractive, glossy, user-friendly manual. The "Getting Started" section is an especially valuable resource for those who want to begin a running program but have no running background.

The Competitive Runner's Handbook enables runners to structure their training using programs designed for each level of competition. Running Coach Bob Glover and his exercise-therapist wife, Shelly-Lynn Florence Glover, discuss all the key ingredients of successful racing. Innate speed is valuable, they say, "but the key to faster race times is the ability to hold a speed slower than all-out for long distances." Glover and his wife recognize eight categories of competitive running: from Novice to the Advanced, up to the Local Champion and the Elite racer (as mentioned previously). Training programs from the 5K to the marathon are adapted to each of these competitive categories (except the elites), allowing readers to follow the one most appropriate to their present level of fitness.

HAVE YOUR RUNNING SHOES FITTED BY A PRO

Each of your running shoes lands on the ground about 800 times per mile. Multiply that by the number of miles in your typical run, and consider how much you weigh. Then calculate the tons of pounding those shoes endure each time you hit the pavement. The impact of each of your steps is transmitted from your feet through your ankles, knees, and hips and can eventually lead to all kinds of trouble if you don't have the right shoes. That's why you need to have your new shoes fitted in a serious running shoe store, preferably by another runner who has been trained in this type of fitting.

The general consensus is that regular runners should replace their running shoes after every 300 to 500 miles, depending on their weight and the surfaces on which they typically run. It's best to visit the shoe store in the late afternoon or evening since your feet swell throughout the day and will therefore be at their biggest ("running size") for correct sizing.

Your current shoes may show the telltale signs of overpronation (too much inward rolling of the foot) or excessive supination (too much outward rolling), so bring them along for the salesperson to examine. An examination of your arch (low, neutral, or high) and foot type should be standard practice in addition to measuring each foot. A good salesperson will also ask many questions, including the type of running you do, your weekly mileage, where you run, how often you race, and past running injuries.

Take a test run in your new shoes while at the store, either out in the parking lot or on an in-store treadmill, in order to test the fit and allow the salesperson to observe your running style. (Some stores now use a special camera to capture how your feet and ankles make impact during a treadmill test to help in the assessment of what shoe is best for you.) Finally, don't pick shoes based on color or style. After all, what good are nice-looking shoes if you're too injured to run in them?

What to do with those old shoes? Read on . . .

DONATE YOUR OLD RUNNING SHOES

Mark Coogan, a three-time national road race champion and member of the 1996 Olympic Marathon team, says another thing all runners should do is donate their old running shoes to charity. One of those charities is Shoe4Africa. For 13 years the organization has collected and distributed running shoes for African youths that have been donated by runners around the world. The organization notes that while putting shoes on a person builds self-esteem, it also increases hygiene and greatly reduces the chance of picking up intestinal worms, which enter through exposed bare feet. Supermodel Kim Alexis and celebrities such as Natalie Portman and Cameron Diaz lend their support to this program, along with many world-class runners. One of them, Fabiano Joseph, was once a barefoot recipient of a pair of donated shoes and later became the world half marathon champion. Its Web site (www. shoe4africa.org) gives information on donating old shoes, which should have at least another 100 miles of running left in them.

Another group, Soles4soles, first sprinted into action after the 2004 tsunami in Southeast Asia and wants to "change the world one pair at a time" with your running shoe donations. The nonprofit exists to facilitate the donation and distribution of running shoes all over the world "to impact as many lives as possible with the gift of shoes." Simply enter your zip code on its Web site (www.soles4soles.org) to find the nearest location that will gladly take your old shoes.

One World Running is a Colorado nonprofit that began in 1986 when a group of elite Boulder runners began collecting athletic shoes and sending them to third-world countries. Most of the shoes are donated by individuals and running clubs and then delivered to various drop-off locations. The charity also holds the annual West End 3K (1.8-mile) race in downtown Boulder to help raise funds for the program. Each $195 raised will pay for sending 50 pairs of donated running shoes to sub-Saharan Africa or 100 pairs to Haiti or Central America. Another road race that has collected more than 5,000 pairs of donated shoes is the Shoes for the Shelter 5K (3.1 miles), sponsored by Canisius College in Buffalo,

New York. Participants are encouraged to bring old running shoes to the race, which are then donated to the local Saint Vincent de Paul shelter.

What if your shoes are too worn for a deserving charity? Nike has an innovative solution with its Reuse A Shoe program (www.nikereuseashoe.com). It partners with the National Recycling Coalition to collect old shoes from more than a hundred Reuse A Shoe locations across the United States. The shoes are then recycled and transformed into materials used for creating running tracks, interlocking gym flooring tiles, playground surfacing, and tennis courts. But if you're thinking about getting an environmentally friendly venue in your neighborhood for those mile repeats, you better get busy; it takes 75,000 pairs of old Nikes, Brooks, Asics, and Reeboks to make one running track!

RUNNING BAREFOOT

Having your shoes properly fitted by a pro is a good idea, but there is growing debate in the running community surrounding the effectiveness and usefulness of today's running shoes. Scientists and runners alike cite a body of evidence that running shoes, with perhaps too much cushioning and support, do more to encourage injuries than protect against them.

PM&R, the Journal of the American Academy of Physical Medicine and Rehabilitation, published a study in 2009 about the effect of modern-day running shoes on lower-extremity joint torques during running. In plain English, how does running with shoes affect the hip and knee joints versus running shoeless? A team of researchers put 68 young-adult runners on a treadmill and had them run shoeless as well as in "stability"-type running shoes. The results indicated that runners suffered an average of 54 percent more unnecessary hip rotation and 38 percent more twisting in their knees and ankles when wearing running shoes than when wearing no shoes at all.

In his book *Born to Run,* Christopher McDougall cites several studies examining the relationship between running shoes and injuries. A study in *Medicine & Science in Sports & Exercise,* for example, found that "wearers of expensive running shoes that are promoted as having additional features that protect (e.g., more cushioning, 'pronation correction') are injured significantly more frequently than runners wearing inexpensive shoes." Another study with similar findings reported that runners wearing more expensive shoes (those priced above $95) were more than twice as likely to get hurt as runners wearing shoes that cost less than $40.

Then there is the March 2008 study published in *British Journal of Sports Medicine* by researchers at the University of Newcastle in Australia. The team analyzed decades of sports medicine literature for studies that investigated the ability of "pronation control, elevated cushioned heel" running shoes to prevent injury. Their conclusion: "The prescription of this shoe type to distance runners is not evidence-based." In other words, they found *no* scientific evidence in these studies to support claims that the commonly recommended running shoes we buy prevent injuries in runners.

An alternative? Barefoot running.

"Barefoot running has been one of my training philosophies for years," says Gerard Hartmann, Ph.D., in McDougall's book. This physical therapist, who has consulted with many of the best distance runners, adds that "Putting your feet in shoes is similar to putting them in a plaster cast," suggesting that our feet become weaker when the shoes do all the work, and more vulnerable to injury. "The de-conditioned musculature of the foot is the greatest issue leading to injury, and we've allowed our feet to become badly de-conditioned over the past twenty-five years."

A similar view is held by the esteemed Stanford Track coach Vin Lananna, who says in the book, "We've shielded our feet from their natural position by providing more and more support." Therefore, he includes barefoot running on infield grass as part of the training regimen for his athletes. "If you strengthen the foot by going barefoot, I think you reduce the risk of Achilles and knee and plantar fascia problems." Alan Webb is a case in point. At the urging of his high school coach, America's best miler used barefoot drills to strengthen his feet, improve his arches, and reduce the number of injuries he suffered as a result of his heavy training schedule.

Roy M. Wallack, the author of *Run for Life: The Anti-Aging, Anti-Injury, Super-Fitness Plan to Keep You Running to 100,* is another barefoot-running advocate. His book includes a feature on Ken Saxton of therunningbarefoot.com, who has never been injured in more than 20 years of barefoot running, including a 16-day span in which he ran four marathons.

What's the secret? Barefoot converts say that when running, the unencumbered foot does what comes naturally: it senses and adapts to the impact with the ground on its own. In habitual or experienced barefoot runners, the foot lands naturally beneath their hips rather than out in front, with the outside edge of the forefoot striking the ground first, then gently rolling from little toe to big toe until the heel gently touches down. This is followed by the natural shock-absorbing compression and recoil of the arch. Therefore, barefoot runners avoid the severe impact of their heel striking the ground first. This finding was confirmed by Harvard researchers in "Foot Strike Patterns and Collision Forces in Habitually Barefoot Versus Shod Runners," published in the January 2010 issue of *Nature.* They concluded that "runners who forefoot or midfoot strike do not need shoes with elevated cushioned heels to cope with these sudden, high transient forces that occur when you land on the ground." They and others, however, caution that more research is needed to fully understand the benefits and limits of barefoot running.

General advice from barefoot advocates for introducing barefoot running into your routine is to start slowly until the calf and foot muscles become accustomed to the additional stress placed upon them. Begin with a quarter to a half mile on grass three times a week at a slow, easy pace. And though it may be difficult at first, try not to consciously land on your forefoot; let that foot naturally sense, strike, and adapt to the impact of the ground so you can reap the benefits of a low-impact running form. The goal should be to use barefoot running not as a replacement for running with shoes but as a valuable component of stimulating and strengthening the muscles in the feet and lower legs. Notably, many runners have chosen not to go completely barefoot but to wear simple, nothing fancy, low-cost shoes or old shoes in which all the cushioning has actually worn down.

Manufacturers have noticed. On the heels of the renewed interest in barefoot running have come various shoe designs to make the feet and the runner feel as though they are running barefoot. Terra Plana features an ultrathin, puncture-resistant sole on their Vivo Barefoot model. As stated on its Web site, the product "allows your feet to be as millions of years of evolutionary design intended—Barefoot!" Nike also promotes its Nike Free running shoe as having a technology that puts the foot into close contact with the ground. Another product, the Vibram Five Fingers, actually looks more like a foot than a shoe, or like a glove for the foot. Vibram says its product "puts you in touch with the earth beneath your feet and liberates you to move in a more natural, healthy way."

No matter which side of the running shoe/barefoot-running debate you're on, you have to be impressed with the most famous example of barefoot running the world has ever seen. In the 1960 Rome Olympics, Abebe Bikila became the first African to win an Olympic medal when he finished first in the marathon—running barefoot. When asked why he ran with no shoes, he said, "I wanted the world to know that my country, Ethiopia, has always won with determination and heroism." Four years later in Tokyo, he repeated as Olympic Marathon champion, although this time in a pair of Asics.

Build periods of stress and rest into
all phases of your running program.
They keep you highly motivated mentally,
and physically injury free.

—John Stanton
Bestselling author and
founder of the Running Room

GOOD BOOKS ON NUTRITION

Fueling your body properly will help you perform better, endure tougher workouts, recover sooner, suffer fewer injuries, and achieve better overall health. If you're like most runners, however, your focus is much more on training than on what to eat, how much to eat, and when to eat it. Granted, keeping up with new studies, trends, and the ever-changing guidelines and recommendations can be daunting. Engaging the services of a sports nutritionist or dietician (www.eatright.org) is ideal but may not be possible for everyone. A good book on sports nutrition, therefore, is the next best alternative.

Although Chris Carmichael was Lance Armstrong's personal coach for 14 years, his comprehensive book on nutrition, *Chris Carmichael's Food for Fitness,* is not just for cyclists. Carmichael helps all athletes navigate through the complex world of protein, carbohydrates, and fueling for performance, with "step-by-step methods for matching your eating to your activity." This he does through a concept called periodization, in which nutrition and training guidance is presented to the athlete across four periods in a year: foundation, preparation, specialization, and transition. This is because the amount of energy athletes burn changes as they go through a year of training. The goal is to teach the athlete to consume the right foods, in the right proportions, and at the right times, to provide the energy needed to perform at optimal levels.

The popular author and sports nutritionist Nancy Clark sees many runners who have the discipline to train but not the discipline to stick to a nutrition program. For them, good nutrition is the missing link in an otherwise comprehensive fitness program. In her *Food Guide for New Runners* and *Food Guide for Marathoners,* she teaches beginning runners and novice marathoners of all ages and abilities how to use food to accomplish their goals, allowing them to train for and complete a marathon or other race distance without running out of energy. In this fact-filled nutrition resource, runners will learn what to eat before, during, and after a race, how to lose weight and have energy to train, and how to manage day-to-day eating—even if they typically eat on the run.

Matt Fitzgerald, the author of *Runner's World Performance Nutrition for Runners,* also knows that runners have their own special nutrition requirements. His program is a systematic approach to using food and nutritional supplements to enhance running performance. Performance Nutrition, he says in his book, is a way to "reduce athletes' use of performance enhancing drugs by demonstrating that nutrition offers a safer and equally effective alternative."

Weight gain or the inability to lose extra pounds can affect runners' weekly mileage and inhibit their motivation to continue running. In *The Runner's Diet,* Madelyn H. Fernstrom helps those with weight problems run the way they used to by "marrying exercise to their eating." Her program helps runners modify both their nutrition and running habits to better address weight concerns. According to the author, even runners without weight problems can learn how to maximize their performance while maintaining long-term weight control success with this book.

If you're still unsure about which nutrition program to follow, consider the practical advice offered by contributor and Olympian Don Kardong: "Avoid any diet that discourages the use of hot fudge."

GOOD RUNNING TUNES

The playlist of tunes you listen to while running may actually boost your performance. In a paper entitled "Psychophysical Effects of Music in Sport and Exercise," Peter Terry of the University of Southern Queensland and Costas Karageorghis of Brunel University reported that synchronization is the key.

Their findings indicate that when athletes perform repetitive movements in time with the rhythmical elements of music, that is, "run to the beat," there is a clear ergogenic effect (i.e., an increasing capacity for bodily labor by diverting the mind from thoughts of fatigue). Stated in plain English, it means that if you run in time to up-tempo music, there's a good chance your body will work harder for a longer period of time. Below are some favorite running tunes contributed by runners exclusively for this book.

"Runnin' Down a Dream" by Tom Petty

"Bleed It Out" by Linkin Park

"Viva la Vida" by Coldplay

"Love Lockdown" by Kanye West

"Beautiful Day" by U2

Theme from *Chariots of Fire* by Vangelis

"Pump It" by The Black Eyed Peas

"Scatman" by Scatman John

"Against the Wind" by Bob Seger

"It's Time to Dance" by Panic! at the Disco

"Born to Run" by Bruce Springsteen

"Run On" by Moby

"Foreplay/Long Time" by Boston

"Breathing" by Yellowcard

"Rockstar" by Nickelback

"Already Gone" by the Eagles

"How Far We've Come" by Matchbox Twenty

"Gonna Fly Now" (*Rocky* theme) by Bill Conti

"Footloose" by Kenny Loggins

"Move Along" by the All-American Rejects

"We Didn't Start the Fire" by Billy Joel

"We Are the Champions" by Queen

Frank Shorter

Frank Shorter became the first American to win a gold medal in the marathon by winning that race in the 1972 Olympics, a victory that is often credited with igniting the running boom of the 1970s. Four years later he won silver in the 1976 Olympic marathon. Off the track, Shorter introduced the idea of a trust fund that allowed athletes to earn prize money in competitions that would be used for living, education, and medical expenses. He has served as chairman of the U.S. Anti-Doping Agency, a body he helped found in 2000, and continues as an active advocate for drug-free sports.

DON'T FORGET THE SUNSCREEN

According to the National Cancer Institute, about one million Americans contract skin cancer each year. And if you think distance runners are more at risk for developing skin cancer than nonrunners, you're right.

In a 2006 study published in *Archives of Dermatology,* researchers from the Medical University of Graz in Austria studied 210 marathon runners and a control group of 210 nonrunners. Results showed that marathon runners presented with an increased incidence of both malignant melanoma and non-melanoma skin cancer when compared to the nonrunners. The reason appears to be the significant exposure of the runners to the sun's ultraviolet (UV) rays during training and racing. The running shorts and shirts worn by most runners in the study provided only partial coverage of their backs and extremities. Furthermore, regular use of sunscreen was reported by only 56 percent of these runners.

The United States' 2004 Olympic bronze medalist in the marathon, Deena Kastor, is a prime example of the increased risk of skin cancer among distance runners. She admits on her Web site that in six years of dermatologist visits she has walked out of the office only once without some form of cancer being biopsied or removed.

The Skin Cancer Foundation recommends using a sunscreen with a sun protection factor (SPF) of 15 or higher. One ounce (2 tablespoons) of sunscreen should be applied to the entire body 30 minutes before going outside, then reapplied every two hours. Note that the recommendation is for the *entire* body; many runners don't realize how easily the legs and calves can become sunburned with the sun's reflection bouncing up from the cement below. But sunscreen does not give you total protection. When applying an SPF 15 correctly, for example, you still receive the equivalent of 1 minute of UVB rays for each 15 minutes you spend in the sun. For more tips, including information on self-examinations for skin cancer, go to www.skincancer.org.

WEAR YOUR SHADES

The American Cancer Society not only tries to educate people about the need for sunscreen protection but cautions them to wear sunglasses to protect the eyes and the sensitive skin around them from ultraviolet light. Runners, like any others who venture out in the sun for extended periods, should always protect their eyes with UV-blocking sunglasses, since exposure to the sun without this protection increases the chances of developing eye disease. If you ever passed, or were passed by, a runner in fancy shades and thought it was silly, well, maybe you were the silly one.

The ideal sunglasses do not have to be expensive but should block 99 to 100 percent of UVA and UVB radiation, according to the society. Some labels may say, "UV absorption up to 400 nm," which is equivalent to 100 percent UV protection. If there is no label, don't assume that the sunglasses provide any protection. Wraparound sunglasses with at least 99 percent UV absorption provide the best protection for the eyes and the skin area around the eyes. Darker glasses are not necessarily better; UV protection results not from the color or dark hue of the lenses but from a chemical you can't see that is applied to the lenses.

Every runner should wear sunglasses during daytime workouts and races, along with an adequate amount of sunscreen. You won't just look cool—you'll look smart too.

WATCH CHARIOTS OF FIRE

For true running inspiration, *Chariots of Fire*, which is at the top of this book's "Best Running Movies" list, is must-see viewing. If you've already seen it, see it again. This drama is based on the true story of two very different track athletes who compete in the 1924 Paris Olympics. Who ever thought a movie about *running* would win the Academy Award for Best Picture?

Harold Abrahams is a Jewish student who wants to overcome prejudice and prove that Jews are not an inferior race. Eric Liddell is a Christian from Scotland who wants to glorify God with his gift for running and inspire others with his faith. Many runners will be inspired by this story, which shows how victory can be achieved through the determination of two runners who remained true to their individual principles.

Similarly, runners and nonrunners alike will take inspiration from scenes of Liddell bounding through the Scottish Highlands and the British track team running along the beach with that haunting music playing in the background. Indeed, many runners include a recording of that Best Original Score by Vangelis among their running tunes or use it as the ringtone in their cell phones. Take note of the racing outfits, training techniques, and running postures that were popular at the time. The movie also showcases the traditional Great Court Run at Cambridge, in which Abrahams and Lord Andrew Lindsay attempt to complete a circuit of the court before the final strike of the college's clock.

RUN WITH MAP AND COMPASS

Runners can be one with nature in the sport of orienteering, which involves the use of a map and a compass to navigate unfamiliar terrain in the fastest time possible. This "thinking man's sport" originated and remains most popular in Scandinavia, where it began as a form of military training. The sport is practiced by competitive athletes, who want the exhilaration of bolting through the woods at top speed, and by noncompetitive orienteers, who also enjoy the challenge and the scenery but at a more leisurely pace.

The object of orienteering is to run to a series of points or "controls" shown on a map, choosing unspecified routes that will enable the participant to find all the controls and get back to the finish in the shortest amount of time. Topographic maps developed especially for the sport are used for navigation and indicate the controls and the order in which they must be visited. Maps also include elevation, vegetation, ditches, fences, and other landmarks. The controls are centered around a specific feature on the terrain, such as an old tree stump, a knoll, or a boulder. To verify a visit to each control site, the orienteer uses a paper punch to mark his or her control card; different punches at each control site make different patterns of holes in the paper.

Runners do not have to be expert in the compass and topo map to enjoy the sport of orienteering. Nevertheless, they should be prepared for the inevitable moment along the course when they become, well, disoriented. Find a club at www.us.orienteering.org.

Find the thing about running you like the most—and when you hit a dead spot in your training or running, return to that activity. For example, a trail run, a run by water, a run with friends.

—Greg Meyer
Past winner of the Boston and Chicago Marathons

GOOD BOOKS FOR INSPIRATION

It's a treat being a long-distance runner.

—*Alan Sillitoe*

"The Loneliness of the Long Distance Runner" is a short story by Alan Sillitoe about a cross-country runner out to stick it to the system. From the start you feel a bond with the main character, who says that "Running had always been made much of in our family, especially running away from the police." Sillitoe has a knack for describing what goes on in the mind and body of the rebellious, working-class runner during training runs and in the climactic race. When he observes that the feeling of running across country "was the only honesty and realness there was in the world," there is a sense that the character truly loves the sport in which he is forced to compete, no matter how that final race plays out.

The Extra Mile: One Woman's Personal Journey to Ultra-Running Greatness, by Pam Reed, should inspire any runner who has to juggle a competitive training schedule with a family and a career. The wife, mother, athlete, and entrepreneur has twice won the 135-mile Badwater Ultramarathon, considered the sport's most grueling race. Other career highlights include setting the women's record for the USATF 24-hour run, and becoming the first person to complete a 300-mile run without sleep. The memoir, however, is not just about her passion for running and how far the human body can be pushed, but also about her personal 15-year battle with anorexia.

Born to Run discloses the secrets of a near-mythical tribe in Mexico's remote Copper Canyon, who, according to the author, Christopher McDougall, "may be the healthiest and most serene people on earth, and the greatest runners of all time." Living a somewhat Stone Age existence, the Tarahumara Indians take enjoyment from running ultra distances over rugged canyon trails without the benefit of sophisticated training or running shoes. The book includes an account of the surprising victory achieved by a Tarahumara runner in the Leadville 100 race, and a climactic 50-mile race through their own canyon country against one of America's top ultramarathoners.

This Voice in My Heart is a story of faith, grace, and forgiveness that recounts Gilbert Tuhabonye's journey from the sole survivor of a Hutu massacre to all-American runner. Born to parents of the Tutsi tribe in the African country of Burundi, Gilbert grew up with a love of running. By his senior year at high school, he was already a national champion with a goal of receiving a scholarship to a U.S. college. When a Hutu mob attacked Gilbert's school and left him for dead, however, his only goal was survival. The inspirational autobiography discusses his spiritual as well as physical healing, as his faith eventually enabled him to forgive his attackers. Tuhabonye eventually graduated from Abilene Christian University and now coaches runners in a program called Gilbert's Gazelles.

Once a Runner by John L. Parker, Jr., has been acclaimed by many as the most accurate portrayal of elite runners yet written. This fictional account of a collegiate miler, Quenton Cassidy, by a former University of Florida track star has been a source of inspiration for runners of all ages since its publication in 1978. As a cult classic it provides glimpses into the running fraternity of world-class athletes, and includes a memorable account of a torturous 60-lap interval training session. The hero's spirit and philosophy are perhaps best summed up by the following:

Running to him was real; the way he did it the realest thing he knew. It was all joy and woe, hard as diamond; it made him weary beyond comprehension. But it also made him free.

First Marathons by Gail Kislevitz recounts how running a first marathon became a path to self-discovery for 37 men and women. The book is a collection of stories from famous (Bill Rodgers, Grete Waitz) and not-so-famous runners who share their experiences in what the author calls "Personal Encounters with the 26.2-Mile Monster." Readers will read what 26.2 miles meant to a workaholic, four-pack-a-day smoker on blood pressure medication; how the marathon distance changed the life of a woman who had grown up near starvation in war-torn Japan; and why an undertrained asthmatic half seriously described his condition near the end of the race by noting, "At mile 22 I contemplated suicide."

USE A TREADMILL

Christine Clark of Anchorage, Alaska, made news not just for coming out of nowhere to win the 2000 Olympic Marathon trials but also for revealing that she had done much of her training for that race on a treadmill in her basement. As she told *Running Times,* "People don't realize, once the snow starts falling, we don't see pavement again until the spring." Of course, training on the "mill" may not be everyone's cup of tea. Some compare it to running like a gerbil in a cage, and many expect to be bored just by the thought of going nowhere fast. Still, all runners should include a treadmill as part of their training program.

The most obvious benefit is that running on a cushioned, motorized belt gives your body a break from the pounding of running on asphalt, concrete, or other nonforgiving outdoor surfaces. And with the new generation of treadmills, runners have the ability to control the terrain on which they run. Punch in a hill workout, a rolling course, or a program with a little bit of everything to fight the monotony.

Another benefit is the ability to set a goal pace for different workouts. For example, adjust the settings to run faster than race pace for 45 seconds and then reduce the speed for a 2-minute recovery interval. Then repeat. Or check out www.active.com for a good selection of workouts specifically for the treadmill. For her Olympic training, Clark favored half-mile and mile repeats, and marathon-pace runs of 13 to 15 miles. Workouts like these also help fine-tune a runner's cadence or leg turnover, since the belt pulls a runner's leg back quickly after each foot strike, preparing for the next revolution. Many runners notice that they run with a faster leg turnover once they return to the roads after their treadmill sessions.

But how does one account for the difference between running five miles on a motorized belt and a "real" five miles out on the road? Experts say a calibration factor is needed. The Web site www .runquick.com suggests setting the incline to 1.5 degrees to better approximate the outdoor distance.

DONATE YOUR OLD RACE T-SHIRTS

You probably have a favorite race T-shirt with which you are not willing to part. Perhaps it's the one from the first race you ever ran or from that 10K in which you snagged first in your age group. Maybe the shirt's design is a work of art that just happens to match the color of your eyes. But odds are that many of the souvenir T-shirts you've accumulated over the years of racing are hidden away in your closet or remain untouched in your bottom dresser drawer. There is no better time to give them away. In fact, many charities would love to literally take the shirt off your back.

Chicagoland Head-Huggers is one of them. This not-for-profit organization founded by a breast cancer survivor accepts donations of unused race T-shirts and crafts them into scarves for cancer patients. The soft, 100 percent cotton shirts make the perfect coverings for the bald heads of patients undergoing chemotherapy.

The Bradenton Runners Club of Florida donates race T-shirts to Hope Family Services, a local organization that provides shelter for victims of domestic violence. Many individuals enter the shelter with nothing more than the clothes they are wearing.

Similarly, the Muddy Moose Trail Race in New Hampshire asks its runners to clean out their closets for those less fortunate. The recipient of their donated new or lightly used race T-shirts is Missionaries of Charity, a group of Haitian missions associated with Mother Teresa's order. "You might not believe how much a simple thing like a fresh T-shirt that we take for granted is valued by people in this impoverished nation," say the race organizers.

Next time you are about to add another race T-shirt to your collection, think about an organization in your community that could *really* use it. Spread the word to race directors as well, since they may have stacks of leftover shirts from old races. And don't think shirts with race dates from years past are of no use to anyone. On the contrary, shirts in matching colors from any year make great uniforms for youth teams, which often lack the funds to acquire them.

Kathrine Switzer

In 1967, Kathrine Switzer challenged the all-male tradition of the Boston Marathon to become the first woman to officially run that race. The celebrated event inspired her to create the Avon International Running Circuit, a global series of women's running events in 25 countries involving more than one million women. Switzer later was a driving force for the inclusion of a women's marathon event in the 1984 Olympic Games. After her Boston Marathon debut, she went on to run 35 marathons, including a win at the New York City Marathon, and at one time was ranked sixth in the world at that distance. Switzer has received numerous citations and awards for her efforts in advancing sports opportunities for women and continues as a popular television commentator for major marathons around the country.

RUNNING BEHIND
A BABY STROLLER

This is for new mothers who may have stopped running due to pregnancy and want to start again. It's also for fathers, grandparents, aunts, and uncles. Actually, it's for anyone who wants to spend more time with the young ones without forsaking their favorite pastime. Why not invest in a running stroller?

These three-wheeled chariots are baby strollers that have been modified for running enthusiasts. They are designed to carry an infant comfortably at a brisk pace set by the person running behind. Running strollers are lightweight and aerodynamic, making them easy to push, and typically come with 16- or 20-inch wheels, which offer superior glide. The Baby Jogger was first on the market in the mid-1980s. Other leading brands are Tike Tech, Valco, BOB, and InStep. One good source for learning about these strollers is www.joggingstroller.com, with product reviews, testimonials, and other helpful information. In *The Runner's Handbook,* Bob Glover offers tips for incorporating a running stroller into your training program:

- Choose a stroller with easily adjustable handles to fit the height of both parents.
- Think first of the safety of your child and not your workout. Walk down steep hills. Run in parks at times with less congestion and never on roads with traffic.
- Realize that you won't be able to run as easily since your arms are pushing the stroller and are not being used to propel yourself forward. Run at about the heart-rate level you would run without the stroller, which may mean slowing your pace by a minute per mile or more.
- Talk to your child throughout the run. Build your parental bond by making him or her part of the run.

"Long-distance running is particularly good training in perseverance."

—Mao Zedong

"Pain is temporary, pride is forever!"

—Unknown

"We run, not because we think it is doing us good, but because we enjoy it and cannot help ourselves."

—Roger Bannister

"Train, don't strain."

—Arthur Lydiard

"But now my task is smoothly done: I can fly or I can run."

—John Milton

PART IV   GO THE DISTANCE

RACES EVERY RUNNER SHOULD TRY AT LEAST ONCE

BAY TO BREAKERS

This 12K (7.4-mile) race, which will celebrate its 100th anniversary in 2011, is one part elite competition and three parts carnival, which is why it also made the list of "The Most Fun Races." When you run it, you'll know why. B2B is considered one of the most exhilarating and scenic footraces in the world, boasting nearly 70,000 runners and thousands more cheering spectators. The course begins at sea level at the Embarcadero and rises steeply around the 2.5-mile mark. The 11 percent grade between Fillmore and Steiner brings runners to the highest point in the race, about 215 feet above sea level. Although it's the only hill in the race, being San Francisco, it's a steep one. Indeed, *Runner's World* magazine designated the Hayes Street Hill as one of the racing world's "Sublime Climbs." The remainder of the course gradually flows alongside the Panhandle and through Golden Gate Park. Thousands annually compete in the highly competitive costume division, while many others compete in their birthday suits in what is known as the "Bare to Breakers" run. But more on that later.

PEACHTREE ROAD RACE

With 55,000 runners, 3,200 volunteers, and 600 portable toilets, it is no surprise that Atlanta's Peachtree Road Race is the largest 10K (6.2-mile) race in the country. The fast Peachtree course consistently draws elite runners from around the globe and will soon celebrate its fortieth anniversary. Numerous bands along the route add to the festive atmosphere of this race that is traditionally run on the Fourth of July. The course follows Peachtree Road through Buckhead into Midtown, then along the Olympic Mile, before finishing in Atlanta's Piedmont Park. Festivities end with the always-anticipated Silver Number drawing, which awards one lucky runner a free trip to a popular European destination. In addition to the Atlanta race, organizers have helped Coalition forces in Afghanistan, Iraq, and Kuwait stage their own versions of the popular Peachtree Road Race every year since 2004 at various military bases. Be patriotic and show up at the Peachtree start line the night before the U.S. race to cheer on the remote start of these Coalition races.

LILAC BLOOMSDAY

This rite of spring in the Pacific Northwest was founded by a contributor to this book, Olympic marathoner Don Kardong, and attracts nearly 50,000 entrants the first Sunday in May. Since its inaugural run in 1977, more than a million runners, joggers, walkers, and wheelchair racers have navigated the 12K (7.4-mile) course that weaves back and forth across the scenic Spokane River Gorge and climbs the infamous "Doomsday Hill." Participants are encouraged by numerous on-course entertainers as they make their way to the finish above the falls in downtown Spokane. Only then can they earn the coveted finisher's T-shirt, whose color and design are always a well-kept secret. Each year more than 60 schools and more than 5,000 children participate in the Fit for Bloomsday Program, which prepares them to run or walk the race while teaching them the importance of fitness, nutrition, and safety.

NEW YORK CITY MARATHON

What better way to tour the city's five boroughs than on a 26.2-mile run in November with 38,000 fellow runners, 6,000 volunteers, and two million spectators? The first New York City Marathon in 1970 was several laps around Central Park and drew 127 runners who paid the $1 entry fee. In celebration of the U.S. Bicentennial, New York Road Runners moved the marathon to the streets of New York's five boroughs: Staten Island, Brooklyn, Queens, the Bronx, and Manhattan. The course crosses five bridges before finishing at the former site of Tavern on the Green in Central Park, and unites dozens of culturally and ethnically diverse neighborhoods along the way. A former chairman of the U.S. Olympic Committee Peter Ueberroth has said that "the best sporting event in the country is the New York City Marathon because people embrace the event." The race has become so popular that a lottery is used to limit the 100,000 applicants to a more manageable number. But here's a little secret: entry into the race is guaranteed if you commit to raising a fixed amount of money for any of the race's official charities. Visit www.nycmarathon.org for more information, including several online training programs for entrants of all abilities.

MARINE CORPS MARATHON

If you aren't successful in gaining entry into the New York City Marathon, the Marine Corps Marathon in Washington, D.C., is an excellent alternative. It is known as "The People's Marathon," since it is the largest marathon in the world that does not offer prize money. What it does offer is the opportunity for civilians to honor our servicemen and women by running shoulder to shoulder with the few and proud for 26.2 miles in and around the nation's capital. After noticing the increased popularity of distance running in the mid-1970s, along with the declining popularity of the military services after the Vietnam War, Colonel James Fowler had the idea for a race to showcase the Marine Corps, promote community goodwill, and perhaps serve as a recruiting vehicle. The field of 1,175 finishers in its 1976 debut has swelled to 30,000 in recent years. The race begins in Arlington, Virginia, and visits Georgetown and the National Mall before finishing at the Marine Corps War Memorial. It is there, before the statue depicting marines raising the flag on Iwo Jima, that runners receive the coveted finisher's medal from men and women of the Marine Corps. The relatively flat course, combined with all the goodwill and camaraderie along the route, make this a great choice for a first marathon attempt. Just ask Oprah Winfrey.

RUN A RACE IN EVERY STATE

The Web site www.runningintheusa.com lists nearly 11,000 races across the United States from which to choose. But there's no rush. Just because ultra runner Dean Karnazes ran 50 marathons in 50 states in 50 consecutive days doesn't mean you have to!

✓	State	Race	✓	State	Race
❏	Alabama		❏	Montana	
❏	Alaska		❏	Nebraska	
❏	Arizona		❏	Nevada	
❏	Arkansas		❏	New Hampshire	
❏	California		❏	New Jersey	
❏	Colorado		❏	New Mexico	
❏	Connecticut		❏	New York	
❏	Delaware		❏	North Carolina	
❏	Florida		❏	North Dakota	
❏	Georgia		❏	Ohio	
❏	Hawaii		❏	Oklahoma	
❏	Idaho		❏	Oregon	
❏	Illinois		❏	Pennsylvania	
❏	Indiana		❏	Rhode Island	
❏	Iowa		❏	South Carolina	
❏	Kansas		❏	South Dakota	
❏	Kentucky		❏	Tennessee	
❏	Louisiana		❏	Texas	
❏	Maine		❏	Utah	
❏	Maryland		❏	Vermont	
❏	Massachusetts		❏	Virginia	
❏	Michigan		❏	Washington	
❏	Minnesota		❏	West Virginia	
❏	Mississippi		❏	Wisconsin	
❏	Missouri		❏	Wyoming	

Do negative splits (i.e., going faster as the workout goes on, not slower) to promote better form and improve your biomechanical efficiency. It also promotes mental toughness and better simulates a race.

—Craig Virgin
Two-time world cross-country champion
Three-time Olympian

NEGATIVE SPLITS

A negative split has nothing do with a bitter divorce, a bad hair day, or a gymnastics routine gone terribly wrong. It has everything to do with pacing. A runner who completes the second half of a course or workout faster than the first half has run a negative split. Training runs that incorporate a negative split will go a long way in teaching you how to avoid the crash and burn of beginning a race too fast.

One of the biggest mistakes both beginners and experts can make is to go out too fast at the start of a race; invariably they have to pay for it later. Sure, sometimes you get caught up in all the excitement and adrenaline at the start and go out faster than you realize. Or maybe your sense of pride makes you keep up with those around you without knowing they are pulling you along at a pace that is just too fast. Conventional runner's wisdom says that for every second per mile you go out too fast in the beginning of the race, you will run several seconds slower at the end. As the exercise physiologist and coach Jack Daniels once advised runners, "Most mistakes in a race are made in the first two minutes, perhaps in the very first minute."

A good experiment to help you learn patience with your pacing is to deliberately run the first mile of a race slower than you plan to run the final one and the first half of that race slower than the second half: a negative split. Once you perceive the strength that remains at the end of the race by being patient at the early stages of the race, you will have learned a valuable lesson.

There are many ways to practice negative splits in training. For example, run the first half of an out-and-back course as slowly as you want, then simply run much faster on the return. Or, for a 30-minute route, simply speed up at the 15-minute mark. Look at that first, slow half as simply a long warm-up for the faster part. Frequent negative-split workouts will add variety and a new challenge to some of your regular runs, help you better gauge your pace in an actual race, and give you confidence for those times when you need to call up a little something extra at the end of a race.

FIND A RUNNING ROUTE AWAY FROM HOME

You're in an unfamiliar city and want to take a run, but you have no clue as to where to go. Maybe you settle for an uninteresting dash through a congested part of town, several loops around the hotel, or a run someplace unsafe where locals would rather not venture. Or you just give up and go down the hall to that poor excuse for a fitness center. Not to worry, help is just a click away.

The Web sites www.usatf.org/routes and www.run.com both have cutting-edge technology that provide runners with good running routes no matter where in the world they happen to be. The USA Track & Field (USATF) site claims to have more than 350,000 running routes in its database, and www.run.com lets you browse for routes in more than 100 countries. Just enter the city, state, or country to receive a list and map of recommended running routes for that location.

In **Chicago** on business? Click on the map for a 2.75-mile route along the Lakefront Trail.

On vacation in **Sydney, Australia?** Do a 7.4-mile run with stunning views of the Harbour Bridge and Opera House.

On a honeymoon in **Paris**? Check out the 8K (4.9-mile) route through the Jardin des Plantes.

In addition, both sites have route-mapping tools to help runners map routes they've discovered to add to the database. Now travelers can find a safe and well-worn running route wherever their travels take them, from Argentina to Zimbabwe and from Aruba to Zambia.

RUN AROUND THE CENTRAL PARK RESERVOIR

Just as Dustin Hoffman did in the movie *Marathon Man,* every runner should do a lap around New York's Central Park Reservoir at least once in a lifetime. The gentle 1.58-mile path circles the 106-acre body of water that is now known officially as the Jacqueline Kennedy Onassis Reservoir. Find it between 86th and 96th Streets, with the main entrance, the Engineers' Gate, at 90th Street and Fifth Avenue.

During your rendezvous with the reservoir, keep an eye out for a plaque honoring Alberto Arroyo, known as "The Mayor of Central Park." For more than 70 years, Arroyo visited the park to run and greet fellow runners and joggers. The nonagenarian, originally from Puerto Rico, claimed to be the first person ever to run around that body of water, going all the way back to 1935; in 1985, he was honored by a New York State Senate resolution for his "50 years of jogging." In 2008, he suffered a stroke, and his visits to the place he loved were disrupted until members of his reservoir running family decided to take turns pushing him to the park in his wheelchair. Sadly, "The Mayor of Central Park" passed away in March 2010. Look for the park bench with the plaque dedicated to him, which reads, "ALBERTO ARROYO B. 1916. 'THE MAYOR OF CENTRAL PARK.' THANK YOU FOR MAKING YOUR LIFE'S PATH ONE FOR GENERATIONS TO FOLLOW."

A short jog away is another dirt path, referred to as the Lower Reservoir Track. This route is about the same length as the main one, but less confining. The course follows the Central Park Bridle Path and takes runners under three cast-iron bridges. Also nearby is the Great Lawn Oval, a half-mile track with markers every 200 meters that is popular with beginning runners.

Other alternatives are the Central Park Loop Trails. Runners can attempt the challenging big loop (6 miles) with Central Park's version of Boston's Heartbreak Hill right after 108th Street. You could also choose the lower loop (5.1 miles), the upper loop (4.9 miles), the central loop (4 miles), and the northern hills and southern loops (each under 2 miles). Check out www.centralpark2000.com/products/map/map_home.html for a map of the reservoir track and other Central Park running routes.

Steve Prefontaine

Steve Prefontaine is remembered as one of America's greatest distance runners, although he never fully realized his potential. When his life ended tragically in 1975 at the peak of his career, "Pre" held every American record from the 2,000 to the 10,000 meters. From his record-breaking performances in high school through his years at the University of Oregon and beyond, Prefontaine won 119 of 151 outdoor races. His rare losses were typically run with the aggressiveness he was known for, including his memorable fourth-place finish in the 5,000-meter final at the 1972 Olympics. During that time, Prefontaine was one of the first to speak out for athletes' rights against the old Amateur Athletic Union, which disbanded after his death. Though he has been dead for more than 30 years, his legacy is alive and well. In the last decade alone, a documentary, two Hollywood movies, and a biography have paid tribute to this talented, cocky, determined runner who influenced many people both on and off the track.

If you feel great during a run, go farther than you planned. If something hurts, do not force yourself to keep running.

—Pete Pfitzinger
1984 and 1988 Olympic marathoner
Coauthor of *Advanced Marathoning*

VISUALIZATION FOR BETTER PERFORMANCE

"For me it was a form of self-hypnosis, reliving the moment the way you want it to be." It's called "visualization," the technique Billy Mills used in training leading up to his dramatic Olympic victory in the 10,000-meter final in Tokyo. Like many sports psychologists, Mills knew that the mind's role in athletic performance is critical and should not be overlooked. Studies have shown that visualization can benefit athletic performance, and it is one of the easiest mental techniques to incorporate into your racing or training.

The technique involves creating neural pathways, activating the prefrontal areas of the brain, and tweaking the appropriate motor skills. But don't worry about the technical stuff; it's rather quite simple. When we imagine ourselves performing an action in the absence of physical practice, like seeing ourselves cresting a difficult hill, we are using visualization. The technique uses mental imagery to train our minds to respond a certain way in a certain situation. So, by imagining ourselves cresting that hill easily without too much effort, we are programming our brain to carry out the behavior when the circumstance arises. As Mills explained in an interview, "The subconscious mind cannot tell the difference between reality or imagination" (www.flotrack.org/videos/play/142054-billy-mills-interview).

Visualization can be done minutes, hours, or even months before an event. Mills practiced it for years leading up to his Olympic race and up to twelve times each day. Use as many senses as possible—the more vivid the image, the better—and repeat the technique as many times as you desire for each event or workout. For an upcoming road race, you can visualize yourself feeling rested at the start, effortlessly passing others along the course, being refreshed at a water stop, and finishing strong with a burst of energy. Add your own detail to each of those images and you're good to go.

DO A TRAIL RUN

At some point every runner should get off the road, away from the track, and onto the trails and mud. According to Olympian Jeff Galloway, one of this book's contributors, running on trails "is powerful and primitive." He says, "Positive empowerment comes from almost every trail run I do. I look for trails wherever I go." A good place to start is with the American Trail Running Association at www.trailrunner.com, which lists places where you can get down and dirty in 48 states.

The Twisted Ankle Marathon of Summerville, Georgia, takes pride in describing the race as "everything you would ever want in a trail run: fun, adventure, roots and rocks . . . and hopefully, plenty of mud." Creek crossings at the Swamp Stomper of Memphis, Tennessee, can sometimes be an adventure, but "the good news is that the water is still, so you won't have to fight a current in addition to wading through." The Ugly Mudder, a 7.25-mile trail run in Reading, Pennsylvania, is known for its hilarious entry forms, which advise runners that "you alone are responsible for your welfare at all times. If you get dinged, please crawl to a point where you can hitch a ride back to the start with your one remaining hand." The race's postrace party at the finish is always popular, "that is, if you GET to the finish! There is a LOT you have to conquer before you get there, including your fear of entering in the first place."

Despite these admonitions—or maybe *because* of them—off-road running and racing have become popular pursuits for runners who want a change of venue. The Outdoor Industry Association's estimate of the number of U.S. trail runners in 2009 was 4.8 million, with 13 percent of them trying the sport for the first time. *Trail Runner* magazine is dedicated to the off-road running community. A few articles in its archives, however, suggest the perils one can expect as an off-road participant: "How to Prevent and Cope with Ankle Sprains"; "Vital First Aid When You're Hurt in the Dirt"; "Blister Battle"; "How to Avoid the Crosshairs During Hunting Season."

RUN UP A MOUNTAIN

Heed the words of the famous outdoorsman and environmentalist John Muir, who urged us to "Climb the mountains and get their good tidings." The Rockies, Appalachians, Cascades, Sierras, and White and Green Mountains are all home to popular races that give runners a chance to run in the clouds. How tough can a mountain race be? When the entry form includes an elevation profile of the course, well, that's a clue.

The Olympian Pete Pfitzinger says that running up Mount Washington is something every runner should attempt at least once in his or her life. Easy for him to say! Sure, you may think the Mount Washington Road Race in New Hampshire is fairly tame because, as the race starter will tell you, "there is only one hill." Of course, that one hill is nearly eight miles long and climbs 5,000 feet! Still, the race is so popular it needs to hold a lottery for entrants every year.

The Incline Club of Colorado asks members to "deviate from the horizontal." It meets for weekly long runs on and around Pikes Peak, with the goal of competing each year in the Barr Trail Mountain Race and Pikes Peak Ascent and Marathon. Membership in the club, which includes the mountain-running legend Matt Carpenter, requires completing four workouts with regulars, who live by the motto "Go out hard. When it hurts, speed up!"

For less strenuous mountain races—if there are such things—you can try the Mill Mountain Mayhem 10K in Roanoke, Virginia, which corkscrews twice around the mountain on the ascent. Or head to the Sierras for the Northstar-at-Tahoe Mountain Trail Run.

Obviously, mountain running does not come without its warnings to potential first-timers. Veteran competitors like to say that if the climb doesn't get you, the descent probably will. Which brings to mind a paraphrase of the famous maxim about Mount Fuji in Japan: "A wise man runs up the mountain once, but only a fool would do it twice."

PRACTICE YOGA

The best cross-training workouts are generally those that are closest to running in terms of their aerobic effort. Runners, however, should also consider yoga as a form of cross-training. It offers flexibility, strength, therapeutic exercises, and an awareness of the body's alignment, which can easily be thrown out of whack by the constant pounding of running. Combined with relaxation and controlled breathing, certain yoga poses help elongate and loosen joints and muscles and restore a runner's range of motion and alignment—fitness goals that ordinarily are not part of a runner's regular exercise regimen.

"Balance," "alignment," and "symmetry" are some of the buzzwords you'll hear or read as you become familiar with the practice of yoga. The Web site www.yogajournal.com is a good source for learning about the benefits and wisdom of integrating yoga into your routine, with step-by-step instruction and advice for beginners. For a strictly no-nonsense approach to yoga and its value for runners, you can visit www.runnersworld.com. There you will find teaching videos for pre-run yoga poses (to loosen tight muscles and joints), postrun poses (to help you recover faster), and other videos that focus on the body's core, lower back, and hamstrings.

Yoga advocates say that with a greater understanding of the body and how it works, you become better able to listen and respond to messages the body sends—messages that could lead to injury if not heeded. And with regular practice, your body can achieve a state of balance, alignment, and equilibrium, no matter how much your feet pound the pavement.

RUN IN A NATIONAL PARK

The U.S. National Parks "have been set aside by the American people to preserve, protect, and share, the legacies of this land," according to the National Park Service. Yellowstone was established as the nation's first National Park by an act signed by President Ulysses S. Grant in 1872. Now there are fifty-eight, the largest being the 13.2-million-acre Wrangell–St. Elias National Park and Preserve in Alaska. Perhaps because there is so much to do in these preserves—hiking, fishing, sightseeing, taking photographs, camping—many of us never find the time to take a run during our visits. Don't make that mistake again. A run should be as much a part of your National Park to-do list as toasting marshmallows over a campfire, stargazing, and applying bear repellent.

If you need motivation to run, find a race. The Saguaro National Park Labor Day Run takes place in the park that is home to the giant saguaro (Sa-WAH-row) cactus—what many consider the universal symbol of the American West. The rolling, scenic 8-mile race takes runners through the famous cactus forest in the foothills of the Rincon Mountains near Tucson, Arizona. For those who would rather take their time to enjoy the view of these majestic plants, there is some incentive: the race's "Glad to Finish Award" in the form of a gift certificate goes to one of the *last five* finishers, chosen at random.

On the East Coast, the Mount Desert Island YMCA Half Marathon gives runners a tour of beautiful Acadia National Park near Bar Harbor, Maine. More than half of the course is run on Acadia's famous carriage roads, built by the philanthropist John D. Rockefeller, Jr. Runners are treated to exquisite views of granite peaks, glacial lakes, radiant September foliage, and rocky coastlines along the 13.1-mile route.

Those looking for more of a challenge in their National Park running route can attempt the Grand Canyon Double Crossing. These bold ("crazy" is another word that comes to mind) runners take off from the South Rim of the Grand Canyon (at over 7,000 feet), proceed down into the canyon, cross the Colorado River, and then ascend the North Rim (over 8,000 feet). Afterward, they simply turn around and retrace their steps, all in the same day. Depending on the route, the rim-to-rim-to-rim adventure can cover anywhere from 42 to more than 50 miles. Don't look for any aid stations or ranger outposts along the way—there aren't any. Not surprisingly, the "double crossing" isn't sanctioned by the National Park Service. According to the author and Olympian Don Kardong, running across the Grand Canyon is something every runner should attempt at least once in his or her life. Though he was once a "double crosser" himself, it's something he doesn't recommend. "Once across is plenty," he says. "It's difficult, logistically challenging, but unforgettable."

"Going to a running school or retreat gives runners the individualized information and reality checks needed for goals, plus fun, inspiration, and a chance to forge lifelong friendships.

—Jeff Galloway
1972 Olympian in
the 10K
Running author
and coach

TAKE A RUNNING RETREAT

Every runner should go on a running retreat or vacation at least once in his or her life—not a vacation *from* running, a vacation *for* running. Think of your old summer camp experience with a heavy dose of running and instruction thrown in, but without the archery, sing-alongs, and poison ivy.

A good running retreat will provide an escape from everyday distractions to a location where runners can train with expert coaches and learn valuable running tips and techniques. You'll enjoy the camaraderie of other runners as you fine-tune your running and attend clinics on such topics as nutrition, strength training, racing tactics, and sports psychology. Retreats are typically restricted in size in order to provide individual as well as team training, sometimes by guest instructors who are world-class competitors or former Olympians.

The Camp Marafiki International Running Camp in Santa Fe, New Mexico, offers runners a chance to "run with the Kenyans without traveling to Africa." Training sessions at the high-altitude camp take place once or twice daily at elevations between 7,000 and 12,000 feet. Among the clinics presented are "Training the Kenyan Way" and, appropriately, "The ABC's of Altitude Training."

Running legend Dick Beardsley and staff help runners create personalized training programs at the Dick Beardsley Marathon Running Camp in Wauburn, Minnesota. The camp features daily runs along the trails and back roads of northern Minnesota that focus on the types of running needed to prepare for a successful marathon. At the end of camp, all runners compete in a half marathon as a tune-up for their eventual 26.2-mile race.

The Jim Ryun Running Camps provide quality training for middle-distance (800-meter) and longer races. The former Olympian and mile record holder gears the instruction to developing the runner physically, mentally, and spiritually. Campers learn about training and racing strategies and gain insights from top Christian athletes, who share their faith along with their running knowledge.

The Jeff Galloway Retreats offer numerous clinics, including marathon training, nutrition, mental strength, stretching, motivation, and "getting better as we get older." Runners may choose to attend in Florida, Lake Tahoe, or Athens, Greece, where the highlight is running along the original marathon route.

Coaches can get in on the fun too. Benson's Smoky Mountain Coaches Workshop in Asheville, North Carolina, teaches beginning and veteran coaches the principles of monitored training and gives them the tools to individualize workouts for the runners they coach. The workshop is run by the nationally known track coach and exercise scientist Roy T. Benson and uses his training book for the curriculum.

So if your idea of a once-in-a-lifetime vacation is to run, learn about running, talk about running, think about running, and then eat and sleep so you can do it all over again the next day, there's a running retreat waiting for you.

DO A BRIDGE RUN

Whether it's the rumble of traffic that radiates up through the feet, the eerie feeling of looking down upon a raging river below, the feeling of connectedness created by running from one landmass to the other, or the sense of urgency to cross quickly before it gives way, there is something special about running across a bridge.

About 1,300 individuals have thrown themselves from San Francisco's Golden Gate Bridge since it opened in 1937; all *you* have to do is run across it. If you can make it to San Francisco, crossing the world-famous 1.7-mile-long span that links San Francisco with Marin County is a must for any runner.

The bridge attracts about nine million people each year from around the world. Many don't realize that the actual "golden gate" is the name of the entrance to San Francisco Bay from the Pacific Ocean or that the bridge's orange vermilion color is known as "International Orange." A good paint store will be able to mix a quart of PMS code 173 for a lasting reminder of your visit on your bedroom walls.

A good way to traverse the bridge is by entering the Presidio 10, which includes an out-and-back crossing of the bridge. The race benefits the Guardsmen, a service organization of Bay Area professional men that devotes its efforts to providing disadvantaged youths with outdoor education programs and scholarship support. Otherwise, you can begin your run from the parking areas located on both the northeast and southeast sides of the bridge, which is part of U.S. Highway 101.

If San Francisco is not in your plans, you can plan to visit the city with the most bridges of any in the world. Sure, you may know it as the Steel City, but due in part to its location at the confluence of three rivers, Pittsburgh, Pennsylvania, is also known as the City of Bridges. There, runners have 446 bridges from which to choose, according to Bob Regan, the author of *The Bridges of Pittsburgh*. That's three more bridges than the city with the previous record: Venice, Italy. But if running across all 446 is your goal, it may take a while; the author needed three weeks working full-time just to *count* them!

Try the Pittsburgh Half Marathon instead. The course crosses the 16th Street, West End, and Smithfield Bridges before finishing at Fort Duquesne, where the Allegheny and Monongahela Rivers join to form the Ohio River.

For those who want a little more bridge and a little less road, the Pensacola, Florida, Double Bridge Run is just the thing; nearly half of the 15K (9.1-mile) race is over water. After leaving terra firma, runners traverse the 3-mile-long Pensacola Bay Bridge and later the Bob Sikes Bridge, before a short sprint to the finish at Pensacola Beach.

Also down south is the 2.5-mile Ravenel Bridge over the Cooper River, the highlight of the popular Cooper River Bridge Run 10K (6.2 miles) in Charleston, South Carolina. First-timers may be in for a shock at the mile-long 4 percent grade that greets them as they begin the bridge crossing. The view of the city from the top, however, should ease at least some of the pain of those aching quads. Ironically, the first-ever Cooper River Bridge Run in 1978 was missing something vitally important: water. While millions of gallons flowed lazily beneath the bridge, there was none anywhere on the course for runners to drink, causing many to drop out from the heat. Apparently, with respect to the task of adding water stations along the route for thirsty runners, the race committee decided not to cross that bridge until they came to it.

•

"A lot of people run a race to see who is fastest. I run to see who has the most guts."

—Steve Prefontaine

"Never are my senses more engaged than when the pain sets in."

—Dean Karnazes

"Mind is everything. Muscle—pieces of rubber. All that I am, I am because of my mind."

—Paavo Nurmi

"Running is my meditation, mind flush, cosmic telephone, mood elevator, and spiritual communion."

—Lorraine Moller

"If you can't win, make the fellow ahead of you break the record."

—Unknown

STREAKERS, UNITE!

Streaking, defined as making a sudden dash in public while naked, became popular in the early 1970s, especially on college campuses. It is sometimes accomplished en masse, like the 533-student streak at the University of Maryland in 1974. More commonly, a lone streaker runs on a dare, as a prank, to publicize a cause, or just to get seen on TV during a major sporting event.

While streakers often ended their escapades in the arms of the police, runners can now get all the exposure they want with no risk of harassment in the B.A.R.E. Butt Chasers race series. This clothing-optional race circuit is designed especially for those who choose to run unencumbered by such mundane things as shirts, shorts, sports bras, and underwear. Series events such as the Running Bare 5K (3.1 miles) in Pelion, South Carolina, the Bare Your Hide 5K in Chesnee, South Carolina, and the Ruff Buff 7K (4.3-mile) trail run in Palmerton, Pennsylvania, take place completely on the grounds of clothing-optional resorts. The only spectators are members, volunteers, participants, and guests. More information can be found at www.nudist5k.com.

For an alternative, runners can travel to San Francisco for the Bare to Breakers run, touted as "the most ultimate nude streak in the world." Bare-2-B'ers, as they like to be called, converge on the city during the running of the traditional Bay to Breakers 12K race for their annual demonstration to "promote the acceptance of the public nude figure." According to www.baretobreakers.com, "Running nude is an ointment for living. It sharpens one's senses and it reveres the dignity and the beauty of the human form."

Yes, but where does one pin on the race number?

If you are not having fun racing or training, then take some time off to do other activities.

—Colleen De Reuck
Four-time Olympian
2009 Boston Marathon masters champion

DO A TRIATHLON

You can run, and run well. You learned how to ride a bike in kindergarten. And if you've been cross-training as you should, you are by now a pretty decent swimmer. Why not combine those three abilities and call yourself a triathlete?

We're not talking about the Ironman distance but about the more reasonable triathlons for beginners who want some fun along with the challenge of completing something new and different. A sprint triathlon, for example, requires a half-mile swim, 13-mile bike ride, and 5K (3.1-mile) run. The "Olympic" distance is twice as long, and there are many other distance combinations offered around the country. Some triathlons feature the swim portion in pools; most are typically in lakes.

The Got the Nerve? Triathlon is a 500-yard swim, 14.8-mile bike ride, and 5K run in Mount Gretna, Pennsylvania, that raises awareness and money to support research for nerve-damaging disorders. The Go Girl Triathlon in Indianapolis is a women-only event featuring 500 meters in the water, 10 miles on the bike, and 3 miles on the road. A good Web site for triathlete wannabes is www .beginnertriathlete.com, which provides training plans for all distances and abilities as well as a race calendar.

Sure, you may not be a Michael Phelps in the pool or a Lance Armstrong on the bike, but just think how many of those swimming and biking types you'll pass when it comes to the running segment! As the saying goes, "You never know until you Tri."

DO A DUATHLON

If you don't have time to train for proficiency in three sports but still want some variety in your racing, skip the swimming and do a duathlon. These are typically run/bike/run events, with a common distance being 5K/30K/5K (3.1-mile run/18.6-mile bike/3.1-mile run). For something even more challenging, the "Powerman" duathlons feature longer distances of 10K/60K/10K. Competitors can enter duathlons as an individual racer or as part of a two-person relay team, especially if you have a buddy who can ride like Lance.

This popular event is held in all parts of the country so there is probably one just a short bike and run from where you live, such as the Buzzard Duathlon in Hinckley, Ohio; the Gem City Bone and Joint Duathlon in Laramie, Wyoming; the Music City Du Run Run in Memphis; and the YMCA Youth Duathlon in Bellingham, Washington. The Fly by Night Duathlon uses a run/bike/run/bike/run format and gives cyclists the thrill of completing their portion on the historic Watkins Glen International racetrack in upstate New York.

Elite athletes from around the country can advance to the USA National Duathlon Championships and World Championships. Two Web sites with good information on the sport are www.duathlon.com and www.runningusa.com.

Grete Waitz

Grete Waitz is a nine-time winner of the New York City Marathon, an Olympic silver medalist in the marathon, and the first woman to run 26.2 miles in less than two and a half hours. The Norwegian native also excelled in shorter distances, having won the World Cross Country Championships five times and multiple victories in both the Peachtree 10K Road Race and the L'eggs Mini Marathon. Her rival Ingrid Kristiansen once said that Grete "showed what women could do if we trained like men." For her influence on running in the United States, Waitz became the first foreign runner inducted into the National Distance Running Hall of Fame. Since her retirement from competitive running, Waitz has authored several books and done charity work on behalf of several organizations, while continuing her personal battle against cancer.

ATTEMPT THE GREAT COURT RUN

For any runner suitably inspired by the Great Court Run in *Chariots of Fire,* redeeming your frequent-flyer miles for a flight across the pond is a no-brainer. Upon arrival at Trinity College at the University of Cambridge for an attempt at the historic run, you shouldn't have any difficulty finding the course; just look for the largest enclosed courtyard in all of Europe.

Trinity College's Great Court Run takes place on a 341-meter course around the four sides of the Great Court, which must be completed in a time of about 43 seconds, or the time it takes the college clock to strike the hour of twelve. This includes the preparatory chimes and two sets of twelve, since the clock strikes each hour twice. According to the college, however, the time can vary due to atmospheric conditions and the winding of the clock.

Odds are you won't succeed. Only two runners have officially beat the clock, and their successes came eighty years apart! The first was Trinity College student David Burghley, who accomplished the feat in 1927 and went on to win gold in the 400-meter hurdles a year later at the Amsterdam Olympics. More recently, in 2007, Trinity College student Sam Dobin rounded the course before the last chime sounded.

Some consider the Olympic gold medalist and chairman of the 2012 Olympic organizing committee, Sebastian Coe, to be the third person to successfully complete the Great Court Run. His feat, however, is not officially recognized by Trinity College. According to the official account, "the final chime was dying away as Coe crossed the line."

RUN A MILE AT THE IFFLEY ROAD TRACK

No runner's vacation to England can be considered complete without a visit to the Iffley Road track at Oxford. The old 440-yard cinder oval is now a 400-meter synthetic track, but history cannot be undone by mere resurfacing. On May 6, 1954, Roger Bannister ran the first-ever under-four-minute mile at Oxford University's track, commonly known as the Iffley Road track. Sure, most tourists to Oxford University visit the Bodleian Library, whose massive quantity of books requires more than a hundred miles of shelving. Few, however, notice the small blue plaque at a nearby track that commemorates the most important mile in Oxford University history. But you are not like most tourists; you need to run a mile on the Iffley Road track.

Bannister ran his famous 3:59.4 mile without nearly as much training as today's elite track stars. The medical student was known for squeezing in 10×440 intervals on lunch breaks. Although crosswinds and gusts that day were not ideal conditions for breaking records, Bannister decided against canceling the attempt. His friends Chris Chataway and Chris Brasher shared the lead as pacesetters, and after three laps he knew what was needed to break the record. "I was aware that I had to do the last lap in less than sixty seconds," he said in a BBC interview. With a little over 200 yards remaining, Bannister passed Chataway and sprinted to the finish and the record before collapsing exhausted into the waiting arms of a friend.

Later that summer Bannister faced Aussie rival John Landy in the Commonwealth Games. Their race was billed as "The Mile of the Century" since Landy had recently broken Bannister's mile record. For most of the final two laps, Landy held a five-yard lead over his rival. Then, in the race's critical moment, Landy glanced over his shoulder, looking for Bannister. "I looked back on the inside," Landy recalled. "Just then he went by me on the outside." Both runners broke four minutes, with Bannister winning in 3:58.8.

Mile Trivia

The mile distance that Bannister ran and the one we still use today is known as the English statute mile, having been established by a statute of Queen Elizabeth I.

World mile record: 3:43.1 by Hicham El Guerrouj of Morocco on July 7, 1999.

The mile record for a racehorse: 1:32.

American mile record: 3:46.9 by Alan Webb on July 21, 2007.

Mile equivalents:

- 1.6 kilometers
- 4 laps around a standard high school track
- 4.2 Empire State Buildings
- 5.9 football fields
- 8 furlongs
- 320 rods
- 1,760 yards
- 5,280 feet
- 63,360 inches
- 190,080 barleycorns

A two-year study of more than four million high school students during the 1980s found that the average male took 7:40 to run a mile and the average female, 9:51.

On a scientifically based table of comparative performance, the marathon equivalent of a 4-minute mile is 2:12:30.

The 1,500-meter (metric mile) equivalent of a 4-minute mile: 3:42.43.

Based on the 1,500-meter speed skating world record, an Olympic speed skater could skate a mile in about 1:50.

Thanks to www.runningtimes.com for permission to use some of this information.

Establish landmarks in the final half·mile
of the race where you want to change
gears (once, twice, and if necessary
a third time) and build towards
your all-out finish, just in case you are
"in a fatigue fog" at the end or are
challenged in a tough race. This helped
me win my first World Cross Country
Championship.

—Craig Virgin
Two-time world
cross-country champion
Three-time Olympian

GET A MASSAGE

If you've never treated your body to a massage, think about doing it soon. The five-minute massages often given as freebies after a race are a good start, but consider a more thorough massage by a professional certified massage therapist, perhaps after your next marathon. Your body will thank you.

World-class runners recognize the value of good therapeutic massages by incorporating them as a regular part of their training programs. Tour de France riders and other professional bikers receive massages after each day's stage to help promote healing. Indeed, a massage helps the body's own healing process by improving blood flow, aiding in the elimination of lactic acid, restoring nutrients to the tissues, and reducing soreness. Other benefits of a good massage include increasing flexibility and reducing stress.

There are many sources you can use to find a good massage therapist. Ask other runners for recommendations, look for a therapist at a runners' expo, see if local chiropractors have any therapists on staff, and check with local hospitals, schools, or directories. When contacting a massage therapist, look for someone who has experience with athletes who will be familiar with specific muscle manipulation techniques best suited to a runner's needs.

A good massage can cost as much as a good pair of running shoes, so for most people it is more of a luxury than a weekly routine. An appropriate occasion to spend your money would be soon after a marathon, as noted above, when the body is primed for the restorative effects a massage can offer. Other times, you can go the do-it-yourself route and learn some basic muscle manipulation techniques that you and a partner can use, either from one of the many books on the subject or from Web sites such as www.massages.org.

It remains a myth that a courier named Phidippides ran 26 miles from Marathon to Athens with word of a Greek victory over the Persians in 490 B.C. Reportedly he declared, "Rejoice, we conquer," before collapsing and dying. Other unconfirmed translations have him requesting a sip of Gatorade and an energy bar before succumbing to the heat.

Nevertheless, much of the appeal of competing in a marathon derives from the image of a lean, hollow-cheeked, blistered messenger suffering for hours in the broiling sun for the glory of his country. Indeed, for many, the allure of covering the 26.2-mile distance is the chance to survive perhaps the greatest physical challenge they will ever face. As the running author Hal Higdon once said, "The difference between a mile and the marathon is the difference between burning your fingers with a match and being slowly roasted over hot coals."

26.2

But don't be discouraged. The track star Kara Goucher holds the record for an American woman's debut marathon. In a *New York Times* interview, she gave this advice to runners who are training for their first marathon: "I think it's important to have patience and give yourself time and plenty of rest. Don't put pressure on yourself. Set small goals along the way and don't be overwhelmed by the process." Countless books offer advice on training for the marathon distance and avoiding the dreaded "wall" at the 20-mile mark. You could join Fred's Team, a group of veteran and first-time marathoners with the common goals of completing a marathon and raising funds for critical cancer research. In 2009, 700 runners competed in the New York City Marathon wearing the orange-and-blue Fred's Team uniform (see the chapter "Run for a Reason" for more about this charity).

The number of marathon finishers keeps growing. In 2009, 467,000 runners completed a marathon, according to Running USA statistics, an increase of nearly 10 percent over the previous year. The 26.2-mile distance is contested in small towns and big cities from coast to coast, with names such as Grandma's Marathon (Duluth, Minnesota), Running from an Angel Marathon (Lake Mead, Nevada), and the Flying Pig Marathon (Cincinnati, Ohio). If you want tradition, there's the Boston Marathon. If you want flat and fast, there's Chicago. The New York City Marathon will take you through the city's five boroughs, while the Marine Corps Marathon will provide a sense of patriotism and a tour of the National Mall. And for sheer beauty, none can match the redwoods and stunning ocean views along the route of the Big Sur International Marathon.

Those who still need encouragement can find thousands of inspiring stories of runners whose first marathon was a life-changing experience, like those in the book *First Marathons*. Or take it from the track-and-field legend Emil Zátopek, who said, "If you want to run, run a 100 meters. If you want to experience something, run a marathon." But beware of suffering the outcome experienced by marathoners whose love for running was diminished after their big race. As reported in a *Wall Street Journal* article entitled "The Fleeting Benefits of Marathons," studies have shown that hard-to-sustain regimens, such as those needed to train for and compete in a marathon, can reduce a runner's will to continue a lifelong exercise program. According to the article, fitness and dietary experts view marathons as "the exercise equivalent of crash diets, with similarly disappointing results."

Fortunately, some marathon finishers featured in the article remained steady runners long after that first marathon. They achieved their marathon goal, then went back to a running program with moderate distances, shorter races, more rest, and less vulnerability to injury. They continue to reap the satisfaction and health benefits of a regular running program by running, say, five miles four times a week, rather than waking up each day to another 40-, 50-, or 60-mile training week. Running a marathon will probably be one of your life's crowning achievements. But the true marathon, as noted in the article, is the exercise program that can survive for decades *after* that first 26.2-mile race.

How 25 + 1 + 385 = 26.2

The early marathon distance was set at 25 miles because it was the approximate distance between Marathon and Athens. It was also a nice round number. Marathons after that were either somewhat longer or shorter in length, depending on the location and terrain of the chosen course. Then came the 1908 London Olympics.

Because the Olympic Marathon was to start at Windsor Castle, the actual distance to the finish at the Olympic Stadium would be a mile longer, or 26 miles. But there's more. Because the British wanted the royal family to get the best view at the stadium, they made the participants run an extra 385 yards (two-tenths of a mile) so they would finish in front of the royal box.

Not until 1921, however, was the London distance of 26.2 miles (or 42.195 kilometers) adopted as the official marathon distance. Therefore, when you struggle through that last mile and a quarter of your next marathon, body knotted in pain, searching desperately for the finish, and thinking the race should already be over—blame the Brits!

TEN MEMORABLE MARATHON MOMENTS

1908   Dorando Pietri of Italy enters the Olympic Stadium first but collapses several times before race officials help him across the finish line, for which he is later disqualified.

1960   Abebe Bikila wins the Olympic Marathon in Rome, running the entire distance barefoot.

1967   A Boston Marathon official attempts to force Kathrine Switzer (registered as K. Switzer) out of the all-male race before her friend intervenes by knocking the official to the ground.

1972   With the American Frank Shorter leading the Olympic Marathon, an imposter joins the race just before Shorter enters the stadium. After some confusion, race officials escort the imposter from the track before Shorter realizes anything is wrong.

1975   Bill Rodgers sets a U.S. record in winning the Boston Marathon despite stopping once to tie his shoe and four times to take a drink.

1980   Boston Marathon "winner" Rosie Ruiz is stripped of her title after it is learned that she actually dropped out and took the subway to within a mile of the finish before jumping back into the race.

1994   At the New York City Marathon, Mexico's German Silva and his teammate share the lead with less than a mile to go until Silva takes a wrong turn along Central Park South. After realizing his mistake, Silva reverses course and eventually passes his countryman for the win.

1996   With several miles to go in the U.S. Olympic Marathon trials, the leader, Bob Kempainen, vomits not once, not twice, but six times and still manages to win the race.

2005   England's Paula Radcliffe wins the London Marathon in record time despite crouching along the side of the road for an emergency bathroom break with four miles to go.

2009   After winning the previous year's race by two seconds, Ethiopia's Dire Tune loses the Women's Boston Marathon to Salina Kosgei of Kenya by just *one* second.

PROGRESSIVE MARATHONS

Progress lies not in enhancing what is, but in advancing toward what will be.

—*Kahlil Gibran*

You've probably heard of progressive dinners or progressive rummy. Now there is a way to complete a marathon in component parts, rather than all at once. A progressive marathon is a series of runs that, when added together, equals the full marathon distance of 26.2 miles. Typical progressive marathon rules require a participant to accumulate a certain number of miles leading up to the marathon distance, before covering the remaining distance in a final race with all other progressive marathon participants. Afterward, runners in the program receive a marathon finisher's medal.

Accumulating those progressive miles can be done in two ways: by running on your own and tracking your mileage on an official form or by completing a series of designated races. Connecticut's Fairfield County Progressive Marathon adheres to the latter method. Participants must complete a series of seven specified races from March through May. After the final race, organizers compile finishing times in each of the seven races for a unique "marathon" time for each runner in the program.

The Frederick Marathon in Frederick, Maryland, sponsors its own progressive marathon, designed mainly to encourage those new to running and exercise. Runners have from January to April to complete 25.5 miles. The progressive marathon concludes on the last Saturday in April, with all participants running the final seven-tenths of a mile as a group and receiving finisher's medals. If no progressive marathon exists near you, have fun organizing your own.

If Team Hoyt Can Do It, So Can You

Perhaps you have at one time been inspired by the father-and-son team of Dick and Rick Hoyt. For those who have never seen footage of them in one of their marathons (including 26 Boston Marathons), triathlons, or other races, their story is uplifting. Rick was born a spastic quadriplegic with cerebral palsy. As a nonspeaking person, he learned to communicate using an interactive computer that allows him to write out his thoughts using head movements. When he told his father he wanted to compete in a benefit run for a local athlete who had been paralyzed, Dick agreed to push Rick in his wheelchair.

"Nobody wanted Rick in a road race," says Dick on their Web site. "Everybody looked at us, nobody talked to us, nobody wanted to have anything to do with us. But you can't really blame them—people often are not educated, and they'd never seen anyone like us. As time went on, though, they could see he was a person. That made a big difference." Since then, Team Hoyt has never stopped.

Though he does not talk, it is what Rick communicates through his computer about that and other racing experiences that speaks volumes. After their first race together, the Boston University graduate told his father that when he was running, his disability seemed to disappear; he didn't feel like he was handicapped. If their story inspires you to use your running abilities to help a person who is less physically capable experience that sensation, by all means do it.

Runners at the Frederick, Maryland, Marathon have done it for years. In that race, relay teams volunteer to push wheelchair-bound people the entire 26.2 miles in order to bring the experience and joy of running to those who can't. The program is called Running Down a Dream, and hopefully it will catch on in other races throughout the United States and the world.

For more on Dick and Rick Hoyt and the Hoyt Foundation, go to www.teamhoyt.com.

RUN ALONG
THE CHAMPS-ÉLYSÉES

A road runner's life may not be considered complete without a run along the most famous avenue in the world. The Avenue des Champs-Élysées in Paris extends for two kilometers (1.24 miles) through the eighth arrondissement, from the Place de la Concorde to the Arc de Triomphe, the monument commissioned by Napoleon Bonaparte to commemorate his victory at the Battle of Austerlitz. The avenue is home to shops such as Louis Vuitton and Charles Jourdan, famous restaurants such as Fouquet's, luxury car dealerships, cinemas, and other fashionable establishments. And though some of the locals object, you may even encounter a familiar hamburger chain.

The avenue was completed in the early 1600s and has been redesigned several times since. One of the improvements broadened the sidewalks, allowing plenty of room for runners to compete with the shoppers and tourists on the beautiful tree-lined boulevard. Be prepared for a slight uphill grade along the avenue going west. If you feel lucky, try to navigate across the busy traffic circle around the Arc de Triomphe, a spot where twelve streets converge. The safer and recommended alternative is to take the underpass. Those running (or walking) up the spiral staircase to the top of the arc are rewarded with an unforgettable view of the city, especially at night.

The Place de la Concorde at the opposite end is identified by fountains and the Obelisk of Luxor and is the city's largest square. It is also infamous as the place where King Louis XVI and Queen Marie Antoinette, among others, lost their heads at the guillotine. Here you are near the river, so jumping in for a dip on a hot day would be an appropriate way to end your tour. After all, the French already think runners are in-Seine.

ENTER A RACE WITH MORE THAN 10,000 RUNNERS

At least once in your life you should experience racing against a huge field of competitors. Not big. Not large. Huge. Say, more than 10,000 runners. Do it for the camaraderie, for the expo the day before, for all the postrace goodies the big races offer, or for no other reason than to see so many other skinny, hollow-cheeked people who share your love of and passion for the sport.

Many runners plan their vacations around San Francisco's Bay to Breakers 12K (7.4-mile) race, which began in 1912 with 122 runners. These days it includes upward of 70,000. In Atlanta, you can join 55,000 of your closest friends in the Peachtree Road Race 10K, or you can get lost among the 47,000 or so runners in Boulder, Colorado's, Bolder Boulder 10K. Here is a partial list of additional races where you can stagger along with the multitudes for various distances:

Race for the Cure 5K, Indianapolis, Indiana (40,000 participants)

Chicago Marathon (40,000)

New York City Marathon (38,000)

Crescent City Classic 10K, New Orleans, Louisiana (34,000)

Marine Corps Marathon, Washington, D.C. (30,000)

Army Ten-Miler, Washington, D.C. (30,000)

Los Angeles Marathon (20,000)

Houston Marathon (18,000)

Statesman Capitol 10K, Austin, Texas (16,000)

Gate River Run 15K, Jacksonville, Florida (14,000)

Philadelphia Distance Run half marathon (13,000)

Brooklyn Half Marathon (12,000)

Boilermaker 15K, Utica, New York (10,500)

TAKE A RUN ON
THE NATIONAL MALL

It has been called America's front lawn. The National Mall is home to the Smithsonian Museums, the Capitol, presidential monuments, and war memorials. Each year it is visited by 25 million people, more than the number of annual visitors to the Grand Canyon, Yellowstone, and Yosemite National Parks combined. Every runner should make a pilgrimage to Washington, D.C., to run on the Mall.

Known officially as the National Mall and Memorial Parks, it covers the area from the U.S. Capitol west to the Potomac River, and from the Jefferson Memorial north to Constitution Avenue. It contains more than 26 miles of pedestrian sidewalks, 8 miles of bike trails, and 9,000 trees. The prime running route, however, encompasses the nearly 2-mile stretch from the steps of the Capitol to the Lincoln Memorial, with the Washington Monument a little past halfway. Nowhere else in the United States can a runner better appreciate the symbols that celebrate our nation's history and honor our nation's heroes than there.

For a good 6-mile run, try the Union Station to Lincoln Memorial loop from www.run.com. Enjoy the experience of running past the Capitol, where the inaugurations of our freely elected presidents are held; along the expansive lawns that have seen civil rights demonstrations; past museums that hold our national treasures; and beside the memorials to those who gave their lives for our freedom.

Since part of the Mall overlaps some of the 26.2 miles of the Marine Corps Marathon route, it's possible that you could accomplish two other goals in this book at the same time: running a marathon and entering a race with more than 10,000 runners.

Do not change what has made you
successful just because you have
a major race coming on. Stick to what
has made you the runner you are.

—Mark Coogan
1996 Olympic marathoner
Three-time National
Road Race champion

ENTER A STAIR CLIMB

As a runner you're likely to eschew elevators for a jaunt up the stairs, so why not get serious about it? Stair climbs are races up flights of stairs within tall buildings all over the world. In the United States, these "vertical road races" are held in cities from Seattle to San Antonio and Hartford to Honolulu. Chicago, considered the home of the world's first skyscraper, has stair climbs in as many as five separate buildings throughout the windy city, such as the Presidential Towers, the John Hancock Center, and the Willis Tower, formerly known as the Sears Tower.

Stair climbs are excellent forms of cross-training since they require competitors to move their body weight vertically, working against gravity. Not only does this type of racing build mass in the quadriceps and calf muscles, it also gives the arms a good workout since participants use handrails and banisters to pull themselves up each flight, a tactic that is allowed and strongly encouraged. A Web site that promotes the sport of stair climbing is www.stairclimbingsport.com. It claims that 15 minutes of climbing stairs is equivalent to 30 minutes of running. This group is particularly focused on including stair climbing as an Olympic event, believing that the first word in the "Higher, faster, stronger" Olympic motto applies more to their sport than to any other.

Most stair climbs are held in the winter or spring, before higher temperatures cause stairwells in high buildings to heat up like ovens. Appropriately, February has gained popularity as "Tower Running Month," according to the Web site www.towerrunning.com. The American Lung Association sponsors stair climbs throughout the country as a unique way to support those with lung disease. One of its events is the Run the Republic stair climb in Colorado, where elite climbers scale the 56 floors of Denver's tallest building, Republic Plaza, in less than 9 minutes. Another of their events is Climb California, which encourages athletes to run for healthy air and healthy lungs and take it "one breath at a time." The average participant in its Los Angeles race needs about 30 minutes to negotiate the 1,377 stairs to the top of the Aon Corporation Center, once the tallest building west of the Mississippi.

The classic, of course, is the Empire State Building Run-up. The 86 flights—1,576 steps from the lobby to the observation deck—carry runners nearly a quarter mile above Fifth Avenue. Aussie Paul Crake holds the current record of 9:33. Unfortunately, for this and many other stair climbs, entries are limited each year in order to accommodate the narrowness of the stairwell.

How does one train for a stair climb? Perhaps towerrunning.com has the best and most practical advice for future competitors: "Find stairs . . . then climb them!"

MAKE IT AN ADVENTURE

As if running that local marathon weren't enough of an adventure, every runner should add at least one "adventure run" to his or her life list of running accomplishments.

The Patagonia Running Adventure is a 17-day event that explores three national parks in southern Chile and Argentina. Daily runs from 10 to 19 miles bring participants up close and personal with glaciers, soaring granite towers, beautiful lakes, and abundant wildlife. One adventurous run that is sure to create a lifetime memory takes you to the majestic Towers of Paine, but don't let the name dissuade you. Sleeping accommodations are in hotels or comfortable mountain shelters. In order to apply, runners must be able to comfortably run 10 to 15 miles in rolling terrain, according to the sponsor, Andes Adventures.

You may not have the legs to dance the flamenco at the end of this next adventure, but you will be able to enjoy the beauty and culture of southern Spain's Andalucia province with runs along the Al Andalus Ultra Trail. Adventure Racing presents a 5-day, 250-km (155-mile) jaunt across "scenic but challenging trails" in the Poniente Granadino region, a relatively new tourist destination in Spain. Each day finishes in a small village or town where the influence of Moorish culture remains alive among the locals. Organizers say that more than 90 percent of the race is off-road mountain and desert tracks, but the route is well marked with checkpoints and water stations positioned at regular intervals.

The Antarctica Marathon is a surprisingly popular adventure run despite expected race-day temperatures of only 15°F to 30°F, even before the windchill is factored in. Marathon Tours says that runners will come face-to-face with penguins, seals, and icebergs along the frosty route. Safety measures require that runners pass the halfway mark in 3 hours and 10 minutes and finish in less than 6½ hours.

RUN DOWN UNDER

If you've had enough extreme adventure to last awhile, how about an easy run along a gentle trail through a lush forest that links crescent-shaped coves of golden sand lapped by azure waters in a travel brochure come to life? It's called the Abel Tasman Coastal Track, part of the popular Abel Tasman National Park at the top of New Zealand's South Island. A run on the track, which is Kiwi for "trail," is recommended by both Pete Pfitzinger (1984 and 1988 Olympic marathoner) and Kathrine Switzer (the first woman to officially run the Boston Marathon), so you know it must be special.

In 1642, when the Dutch explorer Abel Tasman anchored off this coast, a skirmish ensued with the native Maori inhabitants, resulting in casualties on both sides. But that was then. Now your only concern is beating the tides, since some areas along the 52-kilometer (32-mile) trail can be crossed only within a few hours either side of low tide. (Park authorities can provide daily tidal information.) For those interested in longer runs, huts and campsites along the way provide overnight accommodations. Walkers complete the trail in an average of 3 to 5 days. Nelson and Motueka are the nearest towns with access to this once-in-a-lifetime destination.

Bill Rodgers

Bill Rodgers was ranked number one in the world in the marathon in 1975, 1977, and 1979 by *Track & Field News.* During his career, "Boston Billy" won four Boston Marathons and four New York City Marathons, along with victories in the Fukuoka, Stockholm, Melbourne, Rio de Janeiro, and Houston Marathons. Rodgers was also a common fixture on the winner's pedestal on the road-racing circuit in the late 1970s and ran to a bronze medal in the World Cross Country Championships. Bill has authored several books on running and is co-owner of the Bill Rodgers Running Center in Boston.

QUALIFY FOR
THE BOSTON MARATHON

It's a cool course. It's very challenging. It has a lot of character, with
this one very unnecessary hill.

—*Uta Pippig*

You await the noon starting gun with thousands of other very capable runners 26.2 miles west of the finish line. Television helicopters hover while thoughts of Heartbreak Hill dance in your head. You think about the fear and thirst and pain and joy and countless other emotions you will experience during the next three hours or so, just as you did in the race you ran successfully to qualify for this one.

That's right—unlike most other prestigious races, runners have to *qualify* for Boston. To do so, you need to complete a certified marathon within a specified time based on your age group. Up until the 1970s, the world's oldest annual marathon accepted all entrants without the need to qualify (women were permitted to compete officially in 1972). Entrants eventually became so numerous that the Boston Athletic Association worried that the race would become unmanageable, so qualifying standards were reluctantly instituted. The need to qualify perhaps gives the race a certain elite status, since qualifiers know they are among the best and fittest runners in the world overall, especially in their age group. Indeed, since only a fraction of runners are able to finish a marathon each year and since only about 5 percent of them meet the Boston qualifying time, the Boston field may be the elite of the elite.

The historic course starts on Main Street in the rural New England town of Hopkinton. On its way to Boston, the course passes through the towns of Ashland, Framingham, Natick, Wellesley, Newton, and Brookline before finishing in Boston's Copley Square. Heartbreak Hill is actually a series of four hills. No single hill is particularly steep or long; rather, it's the fact that they are grouped together at the most critical part of the race that makes them so formidable. The first hill is at 16.2 miles, followed by the others at 17.8 miles, 19.5 miles, and 20.6 miles.

An excellent resource for runners attempting to BQ—that is, run a Boston qualifying time—is Jeff Galloway's *Marathon: You Can Do It*. Inside you will find 32-week training programs geared proportionally to different finishing times for the 26.2-mile distance, such as 4 hours, 3:45, 3:30, 3:15, and sub-3 hours. Another strategy is to find a qualifying marathon with pace teams. These are groups of experienced runners you can follow on the course who will run the race at a designated pace to meet specific Boston qualifying times. Not only do they run with you, they provide the all-important moral support many runners need to achieve their goal.

One interesting training program for Boston Marathon wannabes is to run Yasso 800s, workouts developed by contributor Bart Yasso in which runners run repeat 800s depending on their goal time for a qualifying marathon—or any marathon for that matter. As he says on his Web site, "I've been doing this particular workout for about 15 years and it always seems to work for me. If I can get my 800s down to 2 minutes 50 seconds, I'm in 2:50 marathon shape. If I can get down to 2:40 minutes, I can run a 2:40 marathon." You can check www.runnersworld.com for more information on this strategy, which many runners have found surprisingly effective.

Four-time Boston Marathon winner Bill Rodgers realizes that the race is the pinnacle for most amateurs and once gave this advice for all qualifiers on their first Boston Marathon: "Congratulate yourself. This is the Olympic marathon for most marathoners. So pick out the spot where you're going to celebrate with your friends that night." Contributor Kathrine Switzer is the first woman to officially run the Boston Marathon. Naturally, she says that qualifying for and completing Boston is at the top of her list as something every runner—male or female—should attempt at least once in his or her life. Need more encouragement? "Do Boston," says four-time Olympic Marathoner Steve Moneghetti. "The history. The hills. The high you experience when you cross the finish line makes it feel like you have died and gone to heaven."

WHEN 26.2 MILES ARE NOT ENOUGH

It was once an obscure sport with a subculture of anonymous but fanatical athletes who loved running and racing extreme distances over flats, trails, and/or mountains. These days ultramarathoning has gained in popularity as more and more runners adopt a "been there, done that" attitude when considering another marathon. Conventional wisdom states that if you have finished a marathon, you can finish an "ultra."

What, exactly, is an ultramarathon? Simply, any run or race beyond the classic 26.2-mile marathon distance, such as the increasingly popular 50Ks (31 miles), 50-milers, and 100-milers. Perhaps the most recognized ultras are the rugged Western States 100-Mile Endurance Run in the Sierras and the Leadville Trail 100 in the Colorado Rockies. Others include the Bulldog 50K in Calabasas, California; the Bethel Hill Moonlight Boogie 50 Mile race in Ellerbe, North Carolina; various 24-hour competitions; and the Self-Transcendence 6-Day Race in Flushing Meadows Park, New York.

One of the kings of ultra running is Scott Jurek, a contributor to this book. Scott has won the Western States 100 seven times, the notorious Badwater Ultramarathon twice, and recently set the American record in the 24-hour World Championships. Dean Karnazes, author of a top-selling book on the sport, has numerous ultra wins and several times has finished a 199-mile relay race as the only member of his "team."

Ann Trason redefined what women are capable of doing in ultra distances. She won the World 100K (62-mile) Challenge and set course records in the Leadville 100 and Western States 100 races that still stand. Before retiring from competitive running, she had won the Western States race an amazing 14 times. Pam Reed, another of this book's contributors, is the only woman to have won the Badwater Ultramarathon overall—twice—and was the first person ever to run 300 miles without sleep. She often runs "double Bostons" by completing the Boston Marathon course in reverse from Boston to Hopkinton on race day, then turning around and joining the regular participants to run it the normal way. Then there's Diane Van Deren, a former brain surgery patient who won the 300-mile Yukon Arctic Ultra, considered to be the toughest ultra in the world.

Don Kardong says that all runners should attempt at least one race longer than a marathon to add to their career running résumé. The 1976 Olympic marathoner won his first and only ultra, a 50-mile race, in 1987. Similarly, Bart Yasso, the "Mayor of Running," also recommends that all runners attempt an ultra at least once in their life. His choice? The Comrades Marathon of South Africa, known as the world's oldest and largest ultramarathon. The race began in 1921 as a living memorial to the spirit of those who had fought and lost their lives in World War I. The 56-mile race takes place between the cities of Pietermaritzburg and Durban and covers five major hills, with the direction alternating each year—the so-called up-and-down runs.

Many Web sites, such as www.ultramarathonrunning.com and www.runnersworld.com, provide ultramarathon training advice for those who desire to learn just how far beyond 26.2 miles their minds and bodies can take them.

RUN THESE AT YOUR OWN RISK

The start of the Pikes Peak Marathon is at a breathtaking (literally) elevation of 6,300 feet, which is not even halfway to the 14,000-foot summit and turnaround. If you want a preview of the first half of the race, just set your treadmill at an 11 percent grade and jog for six hours while breathing through a sock. By the time runners reach the even thinner air above the timberline, they will need a minimum of 30 minutes to cover just one mile. Adding insult to injury, it may start to snow, even though the race takes place in summer. Indeed, temperatures may vary as much as 50°F between the start and the upper parts of the mountain. The second half of the race, the descent, doesn't get much easier, as runners struggle against gravity to stay on their feet and on course, while avoiding blown quads and protruding rocks. To be eligible for a finisher's medal, runners must complete the entire course within ten hours.

All entrants in the Tough Guy race must sign the "Death Warrant" disclaimer, which states, "All injuries are self-inflicted by your inability." Nevertheless, thousands arrive every year at the 600-acre site in Staffordshire in the English countryside for what the organizers say is "a physically challenging, mentally demanding, fear inducing, visual spectacular." Runners in a typical cross-country race may incur pulled muscles, cramps, and dehydration. Tough Guy participants can expect hypothermia, broken bones, severe cuts, burns, and mental fatigue from navigating manure pits, cement walls, flesh-ripping tire crawls, electrified "jelly fish tentacles," fire, and icy ponds along the 8-mile course. "We send people into death," says Tough Guy creator Billy Wilson on a race video, "then we bring them back."

The Badwater Ultramarathon starts at the lowest and driest elevation in the Western Hemisphere, where temperatures can reach a lung-searing 130°F, and finishes 135 miles later at the trail head of the highest mountain peak in the Lower Forty-eight. It follows three mountain ranges for a total of 13,000 feet of cumulative vertical ascent and 4,700 feet of cumulative descent. Along the way it visits places named Devil's Cornfield and Devil's Golf Course. Rubber soles melt, gel oozes out of shoes, and sweat dries before it can cool the skin. From Death Valley to Mount Whitney, the race lives up to the claim of being the longest, hottest, baaddest endurance race anywhere on the planet. Up to 90 of the world's best athletes compete against one another and the elements every July to finish within the time limit of 60 hours. In a written account celebrating the first quarter century of this ultra, Ann Trason, a 14-time winner of the Western States 100, says that Badwater is "more of a hike, a 130-degree-in-a-sandstorm hike, a torture-fest that I don't want to repeat. I like adventure, but this is an out-of-this-world experience." Notably, Ann was not even running Badwater at the time; she was on a support crew.

During the silver boom in the late 1800s, the town of Leadville was the second largest city in Colorado, and was frequented by the likes of Bat Masterson, Doc Holliday, and the Earp brothers. Now it's the Leadville Trail 100 that keeps the old mining town on the map. Locals call it the Race Across the Sky, and for good reason: entrants run 100 miles on trails through the Rocky Mountains, where the *lowest* point of the course is at 9,200 feet. Hope Pass, at 12,620 feet, is the highest point; due to the nature of the out-and-back course, it must be climbed coming *and* going. The goal is to complete the course within the 30-hour time limit, although fewer than half the entrants on average are able to make that cutoff. Matt Carpenter set the course record in 2005 at the age of 41 with a time of 15 hours and 42 minutes.

LEADVILLE TRAIL 100 ELEVATION PROFILE (OUT AND BACK)

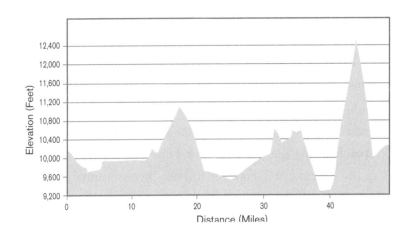

Always include quicker sessions in your training. It is easy to run a race, but harder to run a fast race

—Steve Moneghetti
Four-time Olympian in the marathon

PART V   RUN FOR YOUR LIFE

RUN FOR A REASON

We all know someone stricken with a serious illness or a nonprofit that survives solely on donations. If you've ever run a race for charity, such as the Susan G. Komen Race for the Cure, you should be commended. But if your only contribution was the entrance fee, you're not doing quite enough. There are countless races that encourage runners to obtain pledges from family, friends, and coworkers that will make finishing the race more rewarding both to you and to a special cause.

The 26.2 with Donna: The National Marathon to Fight Breast Cancer in Jacksonville Beach, Florida, for example, uses the Internet to encourage fund-raising among its runners. Race participants can easily create an individual online account to accept and track pledges through the organization's fund-raising home page. Of course, the old-fashioned way of circulating a form for pledging a certain amount per mile is available too. All of the money raised goes toward breast cancer research at the Mayo Clinic and to fund the critical needs of underserved women with breast cancer through the Donna Foundation. The race benefits not only the foundation but the runners themselves. In fact, contributor Jeff Galloway says that every runner should run this race at least once in his or her life. "One hundred percent of the entry fees benefit research and care, and the special bonding one feels between crowd and runners is unique and wonderful. Participants leave with a glow that is not available in any other marathon."

In similar fashion, members of Fred's Team are given a personal Web site where donors can come to make a secure, online donation. By this and other charitable efforts, the team has raised more than $38 million for critical research and treatment initiatives at Memorial Sloan-Kettering Cancer Center, the hospital where New York City Marathon founder Fred Lebow underwent treatment. It was in 1992 that Lebow completed the New York City Marathon while encouraging friends and relatives to sponsor their runs to raise money for the hospital. While Fred's Team members make a serious commitment to raise funds for cancer research, the Fred's Team staff is committed to helping runners train for and finish specific marathons throughout the world or other races of their own choosing. Members receive training tips, nutrition notes, and other advice from USA Track & Field–certified coaches. They can also participate in weekend training runs that are sponsored by the organization. Come the day of the big race, team members can find support by running with one another, all sporting their own Fred's Team uniform. For more information you can visit http://mskcc.convio.net/site/PageServer?pagename=ft_about_main.

Runners can also start their own fund-raising drives with help from www.changingthepresent.org. Browse its list of nonprofits for one that's near and dear to your heart, then follow the easy instructions to "Start A Drive." Your online account will provide an overview of the chosen charity for your race, accept donations, and track your fund-raising efforts.

We all have our reasons for running races: health benefits; competition; a sense of pride and accomplishment; trophies and awards. Next time, find an even better reason to run.

Be Like Bjørn

At the Nagano Winter Olympics in 1998, Norway's Bjørn Dæhlie won the 10K cross-country skiing event for the sixth gold medal of his illustrious career. In that same race, Kenya's Philip Boit finished *last* in his country's Winter Olympics debut, taking nearly twice as long as the winner to navigate the course. But when Boit bravely crossed the finish line in ninety-third place, Dæhlie was waiting there in the cold to offer a hand and a hug. "I told him I was very impressed that he finished," said the Olympic superstar. "It's good for people from other nations to compete." Thus began the start of a long friendship between the two. Boit even named one of his sons after the Nordic legend.

Think back: How many times have you been among the top runners and never returned to the finish to congratulate, encourage, or console someone slower? How many times have you seen the stragglers walking or limping dejectedly across the finish while the awards ceremony was already in progress, never to acknowledge them? Sure they may not have been as gifted, but most likely they put the same amount of effort into their performance as you did into yours, and without any expectation of glory. More important, what if that race for them were the last straw, the result of which might cause them to consider doing something stupid such as giving up running and taking up golf?

After your next race, don't spend so much time congratulating yourself. Go back to the finish line and cheer for those back-of-the-pack runners; after all, you were one of them once. You may not experience the thrill of having a newborn named after you, but it will make you feel good just the same.

ATTEND THE OLYMPIC TRIALS

Contributors Craig Virgin (three-time 10K Olympian) and Mark Coogan (1996 Olympic marathoner) both say that attending a U.S. Olympic trials track meet is a must for any runner. Each survived the disasters, upsets, and disappointments common to all Olympic trials to finish in the top three in their events, guaranteeing their places on the Olympic team.

The University of Oregon's Hayward Field in Eugene, with the famous covered wooden grandstands, was the site of the 1972, 1976, 1980, and 2008 U.S. Olympic Track and Field trials and will again play host to the trials in 2012. Track fans know firsthand that the anticipation and excitement this event generates are not found in the stands of any other sporting event.

For the 2008 trials, 2,300 volunteers helped make the experience an unforgettable one for athletes and spectators alike. One of those volunteers was Nick Campbell, an awestruck, self-described track junkie who said he "felt an unavoidable pull akin to what Richard Dreyfuss experienced from Devil's Tower in the movie *Close Encounters*" when he learned the trials were again being held in Eugene. You can read an entertaining blog about his experience as a trials volunteer by visiting www.eugene08.com/UserFiles/File/blog.pdf.

Many former Olympians return regularly to the trials to see the future of U.S. track and field up close and to relive past glory. "It is just an unbelievably entertaining ten days of action and drama for anybody who loves running," says Craig Virgin. "Many people think it is even better than the Olympic Games themselves."

ATTEND A TRACK MEET AT THE SUMMER OLYMPICS

Every four years you've watched inspiring performances and world records by phenomenal track athletes from the comfort of your living room. The next Summer Olympics, officially known as the Games of the 30th Olympiad, will be celebrated in London from July 27th to August 12th, 2012. Isn't it time you finally attended the games in person?

There were four types of running events in the ancient Olympics at Olympia: a 192-meter sprint the length of the stadium; another sprint twice that distance; a distance run that could range from under a mile to nearly three miles; and a race to test stamina in military service by running up to a half mile wearing fifty pounds of armor.

Compare that event schedule with the *ten days* of track events at Beijing Olympics, once all the qualifying rounds were accounted for. Assume that London Olympics will have a similar schedule, providing many opportunities to be at trackside. And don't discount those qualifying heats where unheralded achievements, upsets, dropped batons, and disqualifications typically add to the excitement.

During this once-in-a-lifetime experience you will be able to see the world's best runners up close and personal, and witness world records live rather than by tape delay. No matter what transpires, you will have something to tell the grandkids one day, and every time you see those five Olympic rings you may feel a connection with those early spectators who cheered athletes running in armor.

ENTER A MASTERS TRACK MEET

Whether you're a former hotshot who wants to relive the glory days of high school track or just a career road racer who yearns for some competition on the oval, you need to enter a masters track meet. "Masters" are athletes age 35 and over who have begun to appreciate the finer things in life, such as good wine, classical music, and, well, organized track meets. As former mile world record holder Marty Liquori once quipped, "Road racing is rock 'n' roll; track is Carnegie Hall."

Masters track meets that are sanctioned by USA Track & Field (USATF) or World Masters Athletics (WMA) can include races from the 60-meter hurdles to the 10K (6.2 miles), as well as pentathlon and decathlon competitions and field events. Hundreds of competitions are held annually, including local sanctioned meets, all-comers meets, and regional and national championships.

Typically, in masters meets, hurdle heights and distances between hurdles, and the weights of the field implements (javelin, hammer, etc.), are age-adjusted for competitors. Many meets feature automatic timing, which links a starter pistol and a finish-line camera, providing a time that's accurate to the hundredth of a second—the only kind eligible for record consideration in most events. In addition, WMA has established a set of standards and formulas for comparing performances of people in different age groups. Through this process, called age grading, you can determine how your times, throws, or jumps rank against those of older or younger athletes.

The Web site www.masterstrack.com is an excellent resource for masters age-group records and rankings, event schedules, news, training advice, and much more. Most important, it exists to encourage healthy competition among older runners by exhorting them to "be the track star you once were—or imagined you could be."

Accept the role as mentor to a slower
runner or a new runner or someone who
doesn't think he or she can walk around
the block, let alone finish a 5K.

—Bart Yasso
Chief running officer of
Runner's World magazine
Author of *My Life on the Run*

MENTOR A YOUNGER RUNNER

Maybe you have already encouraged a young runner into a lifelong love of running and physical fitness as a role model. Or maybe you're thinking about doing so because you wish someone had done it for you. There is nothing like sharing something that is special to you, and that goes for a love of running too. Maybe it's your child who hears you leave on those early-morning runs and secretly wants to share that part of your life. Or perhaps that kid who sometimes tags along on his or her bike during your neighborhood runs would love to jog beside you if only the pace were a bit slower. Alternatively, you can put in some time as a volunteer with an organized program geared to young runners.

One such mentoring organization is Girls on the Run. Through the training regimen for a 5K (3.1-mile) race, this nonprofit prevention program encourages girls ages 8 to 13 to develop self-respect and healthy lifestyles through their running. The main objective is to reduce the potential display of at-risk behaviors among its participants, including adolescent pregnancies, substance/alcohol abuse problems, and eating disorders. With more than 150 Girls on the Run councils across the United States and Canada, there are plenty of mentoring opportunities as head coaches, assistant coaches, and race-day pacers.

The Read, Right & Run Marathon is the youth initiative of Go! St. Louis. It was created to promote reading proficient, physically fit, community-minded children. Children in the program are challenged to read 26 books, perform 26 good deeds, and run 26.2 miles over a six-month period. While most Read, Right & Run Marathon coordinators are physical education teachers, there are also many parents, reading specialists, librarians, and school administrators who volunteer their time. Perhaps you can start a similar program in your area.

Just Run! is a free, Web-based program developed to assist schools and other youth organizations to combat childhood obesity by promoting fun runs, races, and healthy lifestyle choices. Although the program is funded by the Big Sur International Marathon, it is available to any teacher, school, or youth group across the country. Since its inception, thousands of students from second grade through high school have benefited from the program. In California, the program was awarded a Gold Medal by the Governor's Council on Physical Fitness & Sports for "positively impacting the health and well-being of California's children and youth." The Web site www.justrun.org provides information about the program, including advice, instruction, and support for those interested in implementing the program in their area.

Running Rocks! (www.runningrocks.com) is Running USA's resource center for youth running and fitness programs. The site provides a comprehensive directory of such programs and events throughout the country, as well as information on starting your own program, requesting a speaker, and other resources.

Like Bart Yasso, 1,500-meter Olympian Nathan Brannen says that "every runner should do something to inspire someone else to run." Another contributor, Scott Jurek, believes that being a mentor or training partner to a new runner is something all runners should aspire to, partly because the new runner is not the only one who benefits. The seven-time winner of the Western States 100-Mile Endurance Run says that a new runner "will remind you why you run and will fuel your own running."

Ingrid Kristiansen

Ingrid Kristiansen's running résumé puts her among the top female distance runners of all time. The former world-class cross-country skier from Norway is the only runner in history to hold world records in the 5,000, 10,000, and marathon concurrently, with her marathon record lasting 13 years. Kristiansen has multiple victories in the Boston, London, and Stockholm Marathons and is also a winner of the IAAF World Cross Country Championship. One of her most impressive accomplishments, however, is winning the Houston Marathon while three months pregnant, then winning it again the next year, five months after the delivery.

RUN AN ERRAND, LITERALLY

In these days of rising obesity rates, traffic congestion, and concern about carbon footprints, what better time to leave the car at home and actually *run* your errands? By periodically combining your daily run with mundane trips here and there, you can do your part for the environment and get a workout at the same time.

Think of pounding the pavement instead of pushing the accelerator the next time you need to:

- Return a movie to the video store
- Get cash at the ATM
- Pick up or drop off a book at the library
- Purchase a quart of milk or loaf of bread
- Mail a letter or visit the post office
- Go for your morning coffee
- Get a newspaper or magazine
- Pick up a take-out meal
- Visit a neighbor

If you do need the car for an errand, be creative. For example, don't waste your time reading year-old magazines at the Laundromat while your clothes wash and dry. You can easily get in a mile or two outside while shirts and towels are in the wash cycle and repeat the workout once the clothes are spinning in the dryer. No time for errands with that busy job? Then you could heed the advice of the legendary marathoner Ron Hill, who once told runners that "the best way to train twice a day is by running to work and back."

THE ABCS OF RUNNING (YOUR LIST)

Achilles tendon	**A**	
Boston Marathon	**B**	
Carbo-loading	**C**	
Dehydration	**D**	
Endurance	**E**	
Frank Shorter	**F**	
Glycogen	**G**	
Hamstring	**H**	
Interval training	**I**	
Joan Benoit	**J**	
Kilometers	**K**	
Long training run	**L**	
Mileage	**M**	
New York City Marathon	**N**	
Olympics	**O**	
Phidippides	**P**	
Quadriceps	**Q**	
Roger Bannister	**S**	
Steve Prefontaine	**R**	
Ten-kilometer race	**T**	
Ultra	**U**	
Vaseline	**V**	
Warm-up	**W**	
X-Country	**X**	
Yogurt	**Y**	
Zátopek, Emil	**Z**	

RUN A "PR"

Not in the clamor of the crowded street,

Not in the shouts and plaudits of the throng,

But in ourselves, are triumph and defeat.

—Henry Wadsworth Longfellow, "The Poets"

Let's face it: most of us are out there racing not against other runners but against ourselves. What motivates us is not a victory, an award, or a finishing place but the chance to run a particular distance faster than ever before; the quest is for our own personal record, or PR. And that quest should be never-ending.

The term was originally used for the results published at track meets in which "PR" would appear next to a runner's time to designate the best that individual had done in a particular event. These days it's used by runners both as a noun to describe their previous best time for a distance ("My PR in the 5K is . . .") and also as a verb to describe how fast they want to finish an upcoming race ("I'm hoping to PR in that marathon").

In his book *How to Run a Personal Record,* Dave Kuehls writes that no matter how many runners are in a race, each will have a goal that is unique to him or her. "If you ask most runners which of their running achievements meant the most to them, they would invariably answer with the ones that come with no commemorative piece of hardware, only an internal pat on the back: their PRs." Importantly, attempts at improving one's time at each distance are the motivation many runners need to keep going. Indeed, "the hunt for PRs can keep racing fresh and vital for years," writes Kuehls.

Think you're too old, too stale, or too burned out ever to run a PR again? Here are some tips:

- Know the size of the race field: in smaller races you won't have to fight the crowds at the start, and there will be fewer people to negotiate along the course.
- Know the course: a PR will come easier in a race with no hills, fewer turns, and good terrain, or on any course that you like and are familiar with.
- Be creative: race with a friend and try to set a team PR with your combined times; you can have a hilly-course PR and a flat-course PR; you will have a full decade to accomplish a PR for your thirties, forties, etc.

If all else fails in that quest for a PR . . .

RACE A NEW DISTANCE

Variety has been called "the spice of life," "the soul of pleasure," and "the mother of enjoyment," probably by someone who finally ran a race other than the most common 5K (3.1-mile) and 10K (6.2-mile) distances. As the brief list below indicates, there is variety all across the United States. And remember, the best thing about trying a new distance is that whatever your finishing time, you are guaranteed a PR!

Distance	Race
1 mile	NMSU Nearly Naked Mile, Las Cruces, New Mexico
2 miles	Henderson Elementary Fun Run, Woodbridge, Virginia
4K	Sickle Cell Road Race, College Park, Georgia
6K	Worcester Firefighters Memorial Run, Worcester, Massachusetts
7K	Pinch Gut Puffer, Augusta, Georgia
4.5 miles	Bigfork Valley Challenge, Bigfork, Minnesota
8K	Kennedy Drive 8K, San Francisco, California
6 miles	Six in the Stix, Newport, New Hampshire
11K	Greater Hartford 1/4 Marathon, West Hartford, Connecticut
7 miles	Falmouth Road Race, Falmouth, Massachusetts
12K	Heart of Winter 12K, Morton–Redwood Falls, Minnesota
8 miles	Great Aloha Run, Honolulu, Hawaii
15K	Navesink Challenge, Middletown, New Jersey
20K	Lake Monona 20K Run, Monona, Wisconsin
25K	Montana de Oro Trail Run, Los Osos, California
16 miles	Boston Prep 16 Miler, Derry, New Hampshire

"I was unable to walk for a whole week after that, so much did the race take out of me. But it was the most pleasant exhaustion I have ever known."

—Emil Zátopek

"If I quit, nobody would ever believe that women had the capability to run the marathon distance."

—Kathrine Switzer

If you can fill the unforgiving minute
With sixty seconds' worth of distance run,
Yours is the Earth and everything that's in it,
And—which is more—you'll be a Man, my son!

—Rudyard Kipling

"Bid me run and I will strive with things impossible."
—William Shakespeare, *Julius Caesar*

ATTEND A CROSS-COUNTRY MEET

It's the event run by the working-class schoolboy in "The Loneliness of the Long Distance Runner." Olympic marathon bronze medalist Deena Kastor once called it "the essence of distance running in its most natural form." Give yourself a treat and be a spectator at a high school or college cross-country meet near you.

While humans have been running over open or rough terrain since time began, cross-country did not become a competitive sport until the early 1800s in England. Later that century the sport came to the United States, where it was soon incorporated into college and high school athletic programs. The length of a cross-country course generally ranges from 5 kilometers (3.1 miles) in high school to 10 kilometers (6.2 miles) for men and 6 kilometers (3.7 miles) for women at the college level. The International Amateur Athletic Federation sponsors the World Cross Country Championships on courses of at least 12 kilometers (7.4 miles) and 5 kilometers for men and women, respectively.

The appeal of cross-country is running in its purest form, a footrace stripped to the bare essentials; not on a synthetic track but on courses with variable footing and in variable weather conditions, where it's not necessarily who's fastest but who has the most fortitude. Hence the popular motto that "Cross-country doesn't build character—it defines it!" Unlike other forms of running, cross-country competitions are scored on a team basis. Points are awarded to individual runners equal to the position in which they finish and then compiled into the team score. The team with the *lowest* score wins the meet, and therefore the weakest runner on the team is just as important to the score as the strongest.

Most cross-country competitions are typically held on school campuses or public golf links—the inspiration of another popular motto:

Cross-country . . . finally a practical use for a golf course.

Don't take running so seriously. It's good to have a goal, but don't beat yourself up about it. If you're not looking forward to that 15-mile training run, break it into two runs, an 8 and a 7, instead.

—Pam Reed
Two-time winner of
the Badwater Ultramarathon
Author of *The Extra Mile*

RUN IN THE SNOW

In Robert Frost's popular poem, "Stopping by Woods on a Snowy Evening," he was riding, not running, through the snow. Still, because "The woods are lovely, dark and deep," it's a good bet that at least once in his life he enjoyed a good scamper through some fresh powder. And you should too!

Nothing is quite as fatiguing, yet exhilarating, as running in the snow. Your best bet is to accept conditions as they are and not attempt a regular workout. As it is, the run will be challenging enough, so you'll get just as much aerobic benefit by taking things a little slower. Count minutes instead of miles and have fun. Picture yourself running in freshly fallen snow across an open field as in a Christmas card, then looking back to see the footprints of where you've been. Sometimes the simple things are the best.

If you want to take it a step further, you can invest in running snowshoes. As the name suggests, these are snowshoes specially made for running that have lightweight frames and suspensions to allow a natural movement of the foot for control and comfort. Some of the popular brands are Atlas, Crescent Moon, and Redfeather.

If you feel adventurous, consider entering one of the United States Snowshoe Association's sanctioned races, such as Utah's Park City Snowshoe Stomp; the Swift Skedaddle in Silverthorne, Colorado; or the Twin Cities Snowshoe Shuffle in Minneapolis. Some races, such as the Bigfoot Boogie in Traverse City, Michigan, will rent snowshoes to beginners. And don't worry if it takes a while to master snowshoe running. After all, each time you fall down is another opportunity to make a snow angel.

ATTEND THE PENN RELAYS

If you're in Philadelphia to run the *"Rocky* steps," you are just a short run from Franklin Field, home of the Penn Relays. It is known officially as the Penn Relay Carnival, a three-day celebration of track and field each April in the City of Brotherly Love. More athletes have run at the Penn Relays than at any other single meet in the world, and more spectators have watched the meet than any other, with the exception of the Olympics and World Championships. You should be one of those spectators.

First run in 1895, the Penn Relays is the longest uninterrupted collegiate track meet in the country. But it is not just for collegians; about half of the 20,000 competing athletes are high schoolers, who are given the chance to shine in front of some of the most knowledgeable and vociferous track fans around. Other competitive classes include Olympic Development (postcollege) and USA vs. the World, where athletes such as Michael Johnson, Bernard Lagat, Torri Edwards, and Jeremy Wariner have made their marks. In fact, some of the greatest names ever in track and field have competed at the Penn Relays, including Jesse Owens, Paavo Nurmi, Eric Liddell, Al Oerter, Wyomia Tyus, Edwin Moses, and Carl Lewis. Celebrity sightings are common too, such as hometown favorite and track fan Bill Cosby.

While many individual events are run, it is the relays that create the most excitement at the carnival. In addition to the standard relay distances, spectators can witness the 4 × 800, the 4 × 1 Mile, the Sprint Medley Relay (200-200-400-800), and the hotly contested Distance Medley Relay (1,200-400-800-1,600), which Villanova won an amazing 16 consecutive years.

If traveling to the East Coast is not in your plans, there is another meet the same week as the Penn Relays in Des Moines, Iowa, on the campus of Drake University. The Drake Relays recently celebrated its 100th running and is considered one of the premier meets in the United States. Indeed, according to three-time Olympian Suzy Favor Hamilton, attending the Drake Relays is something every runner should do at least once in his or her life.

Emil Zátopek

Emil Zátopek was one of the greatest runners of the twentieth century. The Czechoslovakian was the first to run under 29 minutes in the 10,000 meters and won 38 consecutive races at that distance. Over the span of his career he set 18 world records. His most amazing feat, however, was winning the 5,000, 10,000, *and* marathon at the 1952 Olympic Games. Notably, he had never before run the marathon distance. Zátopek was known for the painful, contorted expression on his face whenever he ran and his seemingly inefficient running form. He was also known for his intense workout regimens and is credited with introducing interval training to the sport.

Instead of overtraining, cut back a bit on the running and do the little things to stay healthy: stretching, hydrating, eating well, etc.

—Mark Coogan
1996 Olympic marathoner
Three-time National
Road Race champion

AVOID BURNOUT

At some point during your running career, after years of intense running, training, and racing, there's a good chance your passion will wane. The motivation to get out the door will be replaced by boredom and the feeling that running has become too much of a chore. Warning signs of burnout may include recurring injuries from high mileage week after week, depression, irritability, fatigue, and sleeplessness, sometimes putting a strain on close relationships. Although Neil Young sings "It's better to burn out than to fade away," that does not have to apply to runners.

Among the main causes of burnout are overtraining and lack of variety in a running program. "Overtraining, in a spiritual sense, is a cancer of the running soul," according to Jerry Lynch and Warren Scott in their book *Running Within.* "It knocks you off balance, forces you to lose perspective with your running, and destroys your appreciation for its essence." Like many others, they stress the importance of keeping things in balance. "The perfect treatment is to fortify yourself with moderation and inoculate your consciousness with a dose of 'less is more.' By doing so, you enhance your overall training and attain not only the psychological advantages of moderation, but also the numerous physiological benefits by giving your body the chance to recuperate and become even stronger."

Adding variety to your running program goes hand in hand with moderation to safeguard against burnout. Some suggestions from the experts:

- **Vary how you run:** Don't always run your workouts at the same pace; try negative splits, ladder workouts, form drills.
- **Vary where you run:** Instead of always running through your neighborhood or on the local track, seek alternate running routes such as a park, a trail, open fields, or scenic country roads, even if you have to drive a ways to find them.
- **Take days, weeks, even a month off** to recharge.

- **Run more frequently with others,** either with a partner or a group. Or, if running with others is your norm, run more often by yourself and enjoy some solitude.
- **Make running fun:** Turn a workout with a partner into a contest or a game; do your errands on the run; try backward running.
- **Add cross-training** if it is not already a component of your running program.

Be prudent in adding moderation and variety into your running schedule, avoid overtraining, and realize that running should not rule your life but enrich it.

The late Steve Prefontaine's fourth-place finish in the Munich Olympic's 5,000-meter final remains a testament to the courage and fortitude to which all distance runners aspire. His age and lack of international racing experience made him an underdog in the 13-man field, but to him, none of that mattered. Consistent with his aggressive approach to all his races, he knew that if he didn't win, he would surely make the winner earn the gold medal. "Somebody may beat me," he said back then. "But they're going to have to bleed to do it."

PRE

The YouTube video at www.youtube.com/watch?v=cGT1xUX3jhs shows that with four laps remaining, Prefontaine took the lead and upped the pace, eventually dropping most of the other runners. With two laps to go, Lasse Virén of Finland went ahead briefly before Prefontaine reasserted his place at the front. With one lap remaining, Virén moved into first place, while Prefontaine fell back with Mohammed Gammoudi of Tunisia. Prefontaine surged in the backstretch, trying to regain the lead, and once again in the final straight, going for the gold instead of perhaps saving what little he had left for the silver or bronze.

Each time his aggressive move was answered by Virén and Gammoudi. With nothing left, he staggered the final few meters, totally spent, and was nipped at the finish for the bronze by the late-charging Ian Stewart of Great Britain. Sadly, the great Steve Prefontaine, known as "Pre" by his adoring legion of fans, died before getting the chance to compete in the 1976 Montreal Olympics.

MAKE A PILGRIMAGE TO PRE'S ROCK

At one time Steve Prefontaine held every American distance record from 2,000 to 10,000 meters. After his valiant fourth-place finish in the 1972 Olympic 5,000-meter race, the experts agreed that with more international experience he'd be a favorite to win that race at the 1976 Olympics four years later. But one evening leading up to that Olympics, he failed to negotiate a sharp turn in the road on his way home. His MGB rolled over on top of him, crushing him to death before help could arrive.

On a roadside boulder at the accident scene along Skyline Boulevard near the University of Oregon is a simple sentiment:

PRE
5-30-75
R.I.P.

Below the boulder is a memorial to the popular running legend and cult hero where fans leave personal objects and offerings such as poems and photos, race numbers and singlets, running shoes and caps, medals and trophies, sports drinks and energy bars.

Contributor Jeff Galloway on Steve Prefontaine: "Thousands of elite U.S. athletes have come and gone, but none have exuded the excitement of Pre. He was a good friend and inspired all of us to do our best." Every runner should visit Pre's Rock at least once in their life.

RUN A RACE IN THE MIDDLE OF THE PACK

The late Fred Lebow, the founder of the New York City Marathon, once said, "In running, it doesn't matter whether you come in first, in the middle of the pack, or last. You can say 'I have finished.' There is a lot of satisfaction in that."

Christopher Russell, the author of the book *The Mid-Packer's Lament,* is a confirmed middle-of-the-pack runner. To determine if you're one too, he says to "look at the results of the last big local 5K race you ran. Throw out the top 10 percent of each age group. Then, throw out the slowest 10 percent." Those remaining are the "serious, but average runners who fill out the midsection of our sport."

The middle of the pack in any race, according to Russell, "contains has-beens, never-were's, and a few will-be's." It includes those who were good runners in school but have succumbed to injury or old age, those who always ran but were just never that fast, and those new to the sport or castoffs from other sports. Although this special fraternity of runners doesn't expect to win any trophies, they train just as hard and with as much passion as those in the upper tier and run for the accomplishment of saying, "I have finished."

If you typically run in the lead pack and have a collection of running trophies on your bookshelf to show for it, you need to run a race in the middle of the pack at least once. Immerse yourself in their world. Encourage them. Pace them. Give them advice if they ask for it. Most of all, listen to their stories in order to get to know these runners, with whom you've probably never before spoken. If you are a middle-of-the-pack runner, run at least one race with those in the slowest group. You'll learn that every race has many winners, not just the one who crosses the finish line first.

If Trisha and David Can Do It, So Can You

During a run in Central Park in 1989, Trisha Meili was attacked, raped, and left for dead. Her recovery was slow; brain damage meant she had to relearn how to do simple things, such as identifying objects, telling time, and dressing herself. She joined the Achilles Track Club, which was established to encourage disabled people to participate in long-distance running, and with their help was able to complete the New York City Marathon in 1995. In 2003, she told her amazing story of survival in the bestselling memoir *I Am the Central Park Jogger: A Story of Hope and Possibility.*

When David Paterson was an infant, an infection caused the complete loss of sight in one eye and 20/400 vision in the other. Therefore, out of his "good" eye he was able to see at 20 feet what someone else could see at 400. David began running with the Achilles Track Club in 1998 as a visually impaired member. After a few months of training, he could run five miles comfortably and in 1999 was also able to complete the New York City Marathon.

Trisha Meili stayed with the Achilles organization and later became board chair. David Peterson became an Achilles board member and was eventually sworn in as the fifty-fifth governor of New York. In 2004 and 2005, Trisha joined up with David, and together they ran the Hope & Possibility 5K in Central Park.

RACE ON YOUR BIRTHDAY

Going for a run on your birthday is a no-brainer. It's an annual present to yourself to commemorate the day of your birth, because all runners know what the Renaissance-era poet Samuel Daniel meant when he said, "This is the thing I was born to do."

Why not take it a step further and *race* on your special day? Not only will you receive a T-shirt with your very own birth date on it, but if your birthday happens to place you into a new decade, say from 39 to 40, you'll have a pretty good shot at winning an age-group trophy as one of the "younger" ones competing in your group.

Finding a race nearby on your birthday may not be that easy if you were born in late January and you reside in Montana. But maybe you can do what Ron Hill did: run on your birthday in a race given in your honor. When Ron turned 70, friends organized a 5K (3.1-mile) race as a tribute to this former European marathon champion and current holder of the world's longest consecutive running streak. The British runner traveled 20 miles from his home for the race, which attracted nearly 500 appreciative entrants. How did he do? Ron finished in 331st place with a time of 26:02; not bad for a guy seven decades old. And not a bad way to pick up another age-group trophy, either.

VOLUNTEER AT A RACE

Race day is finally here. You awake extremely early and eat well because it's a long race; you'll be on your feet the whole time. You arrive before most of the runners, but chances are you'll still be out on the course long after they have finished. You are just one face in a sea of thousands, and few people, if any, will even acknowledge your presence. You get butterflies wondering if all the work has prepared you for what's to come because you don't want to be the weak link; you don't want to disappoint your team. But you're not a runner. No. You're a race-day volunteer.

Volunteers are the unsung heroes of any organized race. Simply put, there would be no race without those individuals who would rather give than receive. And it's not just about handing out water either. Just look at a partial list of the volunteer opportunities at the Salt Lake City Marathon:

- **Registration:** Assist with registration materials and packet pickup.
- **Course setup:** Drop off supplies at aid stations. Place mile markers, set up course signage, place barricades/cones, and remove after race.
- **Aid station:** Groups of 20 needed. Must be qualified.
- **Gear bag duty:** Assist runners with items to be put in bags, label bags, transport bags to the finish line, aid runners in locating their bags.
- **Race start:** Setup of starting line, help with runner/crowd control, tear down starting line.
- **Course safety:** Ensure safety of event participants in heavy traffic areas.
- **Race traffic:** Direct runners around course and down finish lanes.
- **Finish line:** Prepackage refreshment bags for runners. Set up finish-line area, medical tents and chip guider/collectors, pass out water and heat sheets to finishers, chip removal.
- **Massage:** Give free massages to marathoners (must be licensed).
- **Medical:** Doctors, nurses, EMTs, etc., are needed at finish.

- **Awards:** Set up awards tent, awards, display, distribute medals to winners.
- **Postevents:** Cleanup of finish-line festival area after participants have left.

Many popular races have a volunteers link on their Web sites for those who want to sign up. The link at the Marine Corps Marathon Web site offers volunteers "a great way to get in the race day trenches with the Marines." The New York City Marathon Web site lists a wide range of volunteer assignments along with a description of each. "Most go through our Web site and sign up there," says Edwin Ortiz, Jr., assistant manager for volunteers and community outreach for New York Road Runners, the group behind the New York City Marathon and other races. "As long as they are over 14, we accept volunteers of all shapes and sizes and backgrounds. We also get a large amount of groups—whether from high schools, colleges, large corporations, or small community organizations—who volunteer for us as part of their community service requirements."

Don't wait too long to inquire about volunteer opportunities; though smaller local races may be willing to accept volunteers up until the night before the race, larger races sometimes need commitments weeks before the big day. "Our ideal volunteer," says Ortiz, "is someone who is willing to do anything to help our organization succeed at that week's race." That includes the job of race marshal, an assignment he says is the most difficult to fill. "It's not the most fun thing to do because it involves telling people to either keep moving or to not go to a certain spot, but it is a necessary position in order to maintain order at our events."

At a recent New York City Marathon, 6,000 people volunteered to help 38,000 runners navigate safely through the city's five boroughs. "That seemed to be enough to get the job done," says Ortiz, "but we could always use more."

One of the most important things for
a runner of any ability to do is to set
goals for each season. Whether the goal
is to finish your first 5K without walking,
or running a new personal best,
have a goal to work for and make sure
you reward yourself when you reach
your goal.

—Nathan Brannen
NCAA 800-meter champion
2008 Olympian in the 1,500

JUST DO IT

Despite all the advice and recommendations in this book to encourage and inspire your passion for running, there will invariably be times when you will need to fight the demons or other forces that are working to keep you from slipping on the running shoes and heading out the door. No, it's not runner's burnout but those few occasions when a run is scheduled and you just don't feel quite up to it. Many runners will tell you, however, that some of their best runs have come after they initially dragged their feet and thought of skipping a run altogether, before going out and doing it.

That's not to say you should ignore a severe cold or other illness, run with an injury, or go out when your body is telling you to take a day off. It's about those times when for one reason or another you just don't feel in the mood. Two-time Olympian and indoor mile champion Shayne Culpepper knows that feeling. Her response when she's not in the mood is to go out earlier than usual, before she can think too much about it. As she once told an interviewer, "If I have that extra cup of coffee or I wait an extra half hour, it becomes too torturous."

There are two things to remember. First, if you aren't in a good mood before you start, a run will usually fix it. And whether it's the serotonin levels that rise, the endorphins that are released, or because you are doing something you really love, you will most likely feel much better after a run than before it.

Running legend Ted Corbitt had the right attitude. The ultra runner and 1952 Olympic marathoner was known for his 200-mile training weeks and therefore rarely needed a kick in the butt to get him out the door. To him, it was all pretty simple. "Running is something you just do," he said in *First Marathons.* "You don't need a goal. You don't need a race. You don't need the hype of a so-called fitness craze. All you need is a cheap pair of shoes and some time; the rest will follow."

Haile Gebrselassie

Haile Gebrselassie was the quintessential African schoolboy runner who really *did* run six miles back and forth to school each day from the family farm at high altitude. He is considered by many to be the best distance runner ever, with a distinguished career that is a testament to his versatility. The Ethiopian runner has achieved major international success in cross-country, outdoor track and indoor track, and on the road-racing circuit, in distances from the 1,500 to the marathon. Along the way he has won eight Olympic and World Championship gold medals and set 26 world records. In 2000, he became only the third man in history to successfully defend an Olympic 10,000-meter title. Eight years later, at the age of 35, he won the Berlin Marathon with a world-record time of 2:03:59, the first ever sub-2:04 marathon.

TAKE WALK BREAKS

Have you ever run past a fellow competitor during a race who was walking, only to have that person pass you at the end of the race at a full run? According to Olympian and running coach Jeff Galloway, runners who take walk breaks during a race are often the ones who pick up speed during the last part of a race when everyone else is slowing down. What gives?

The Web site www.jeffgalloway.com informs us that walk breaks allow runners to shift back and forth between walking and running muscles to help distribute the workload. Therefore, the running muscles are less likely to become fatigued, while overall performance capacity improves. Galloway notes that even veteran runners have posted faster times with this strategy. Plus there's the mental benefit of breaking up the race or training run into segments: knowing that a 1-minute walking break is coming after every 2 miles or so can make a 10-mile race seem less formidable.

The Web site gives information on how often and how long the walk breaks should be, depending on the distance and your ability. Galloway says that once a runner finds the ideal ratio of running and walking for a given distance, walk breaks allow him or her to stay strong all the way to the finish line, while enjoying the same conditioning benefit he or she would have received by running without that break. Furthermore, he adds, "walk breaks will significantly speed up recovery because there is less damage to repair. The early walk breaks erase fatigue, and the later walk breaks will reduce or eliminate overuse muscle breakdown."

A similar strategy is John Stanton's 10:1 Training Concept. John, a contributor to this book, was once an out-of-shape, overweight, two-pack-a-day smoker who decided to change his lifestyle and begin a running program. Since then he founded the Running Room (see www.runningroom.com) and became a bestselling Canadian author of six books on running. In the 10:1 Training Concept, a runner runs for 10 minutes and walks for 1. John's Running Room clinics have helped hundreds of people with no exercise background complete marathons using this type of walk break in their training.

RUN ON HALLOWED GROUND

Running on an American battlefield can be more than just a race, it can be an appropriate way to express our indebtedness and gratitude to the ones who came before us. Our brave forefathers fought and died to guarantee life, liberty, and the pursuit of happiness here at home, and we all know that the pursuit of happiness includes the sport of running.

The Spirit of Gettysburg run is one of only a few road races permitted on National Military Park roads. The 5K (3.1-mile) route tours sites of the first day's battle, when Confederate troops attacked the Union cavalry position on McPherson Ridge, west of town. Later that day the Union soldiers set up defenses along Cemetery Ridge, where they survived the fierce assault of Pickett's charge two days later.

The Valley Forge Revolutionary 5-Mile Run follows a challenging course through scenic Valley Forge National Historical Park, about 45 minutes outside Philadelphia. Participants will run by the fields where Washington's men were drilled into a disciplined fighting force and the cabins where they attempted (many unsuccessfully) to survive the severe winter of 1777 without adequate supplies.

The Yorktown Battlefield Run takes place entirely on the Yorktown Battlefield tour roads, with scenic views of woods, meadows, fields, and creeks. The 10-mile race begins at historic Surrender Field, where Cornwallis surrendered to Washington, effectively ending the Revolutionary War.

For a crash course in Civil War history and a visit to some famous memorials, the American Odyssey Relay may be your race. That is, if you like traveling in a cramped van with 11 smelly relay teammates for 24 hours and 200 miles. On the way you'll visit the Gettysburg and Antietam Battlefields, Harpers Ferry, and the C&O Canal before arriving in the nation's capital. The finish will take you along the National Mall, a must-run for any runner that was detailed earlier in this book.

ORGANIZE YOUR OWN RACE

Organizing a race for your local school, church, or other charity can be a fun and profitable way of encouraging running among all ages in your community. It's nothing to take lightly, however. Race directing is much more than putting the word out, plotting a course, erecting a finishing-line banner, and handing out trophies. Think of it like that big race you trained for: it will be a monumental challenge, but with the right amount of planning, it can be a huge success.

Giving yourself enough time (at least six to nine months before race day) is perhaps the most important factor. Then, in no particular order, you need to: choose a name and a time for the race, select a charity, settle on the course and distance, create a budget and a promotional plan, secure sponsors, obtain permission, insurance, and police coordination, hire race timers, order bib numbers, T-shirts, and trophies, consider environment-friendly initiatives, and recruit as many volunteers as possible.

Fortunately, help is out there. A good first step is to contact race directors from other races in your vicinity for their advice and guidance. Web sites such as www.runtheplanet.com and www.rrm.com also provide valuable information for budding race directors. *Runner's World* offers the Runner's World Race Series at www.runnersworld.com, a free service that assists in organizing and promoting your race. It also provides free race supplies, such as bib numbers and drawstring bags, product samples, and coupons for distribution to race participants. Additional help comes from www.runningintheusa .com, which offers free Web site hosting for your race.

If the above seems daunting, realize that it all gets easier the second time around. And haven't you always wanted to shoot off a starting gun? Just don't be surprised if you find that running a race is more of a challenge than running *in* a race.

BE AN ACHILLES TRACK CLUB VOLUNTEER RUNNER

In January 1983, seven individuals with disabilities who had been working out as part of an eight-week running clinic ran their first 6-mile race in New York's Central Park. Later that year, six of them completed the New York City Marathon.

That was the beginning of the Achilles Track Club, which now has 40 chapters in the United States and more than 100 chapters on six continents. The club was established "to encourage disabled people to participate in long-distance running with the general public," using the sport as a vehicle for positive social and individual change. By doing so, the nonprofit organization furthers its mission "to enable people with all types of disabilities to participate in mainstream athletics, to promote personal achievement, enhanced self-esteem, and the lowering of barriers between people." The organization was founded by its current president, Dick Traum, an above-the-knee amputee marathoner.

The Achilles Track Club includes people with all kinds of disabilities who compete with crutches, in wheelchairs, or on prostheses. It is mainly through biweekly workouts that these members receive support, training, and technical expertise. The workouts, however, would not be possible without volunteer runners. Volunteers are not expected to be elite runners or health and nutrition experts. Instead, the organization looks for those who are friendly and considerate and want to share their joy of running with others. Perhaps the volunteer's main role, however, is that of a companion who will have the patience to attend to a member's medical, physical, and safety needs.

Besides weekday-evening and weekend-morning workouts, the organization is involved in many local and national running events in which members compete alongside a volunteer runner. For example, each year a large number of disabled runners are sponsored for the running of the New York City Marathon. Since that first race in 1983, more than a thousand Achilles athletes have completed the marathon.

Visit www.achillesinternational.org for an overview of the volunteer program and to find the Achilles Track Club chapter nearest you.

Make sure you are enjoying running!

—Suzy Favor Hamilton
Three-time Olympian in the 1,500

RUN FOR FUN

Think back to the first time you realized that running had ceased to be just something you did and had become part of who you were. Don't lose that feeling. Too often, it seems, we look at running like a business, solely as a means to an end. We get caught up in mileage tallies, speed workouts, the length of our long runs, hill training, pace charts, and heart rate monitors, in order to prepare as best we can for some race on the distant horizon.

Not that there's anything wrong with that. But if we get agitated when we miss a scheduled run, or when our daily, weekly, or monthly mileage falls short of some arbitrary goal, or when we don't achieve our intended finishing time in a race, it's time to step back and chill out. Ultra runner Pam Reed says she sees it often on the starting line of popular races—runners obsessing about pacing and finishing times instead of just enjoying the overall running experience. "Most of them are not professional runners," she says. "They have lives and jobs. Once in a while they need to just take it all in and enjoy it. Running is supposed to be fun."

Competitors in San Francisco's Bay to Breakers race have the right idea, as we've noted previously. Organizers describe the race as "a glorious celebration of the human spirit—a giant wave of athleticism, fun, frivolity, and determination flowing across the city." That should be our goal for the majority of our running experiences: to run not for the sake of building a mileage base, nor for how fast or how far, but simply for the sheer fun of it.

Brian Sell knows how to run for fun. In the foreword to this book, the Olympian recalled that many of the best experiences of his life occurred when he was running. And even though his competitive career is coming to an end, he still looks upon every run as a treasure. "I plan to run for the rest of my life," he says. "It will always be part of who I am."

BELIEVE YOU'RE NEVER TOO OLD TO RUN

You don't stop running because you get old. You get old because you stop running.

—*Common runner's saying*

Studies have shown that as our years increase, our coordination, reaction time, muscle strength, and ability to efficiently use oxygen all decrease. We also know that the older we get, the more easily we can become injured and the more time we need to heal from those injuries. Wouldn't it be nice if there were something we could do today that would slow the effects of aging and give us extra tomorrows? Well, there is. It's called running.

A 2009 study by a team of German scientists, for example, shed light on running's antiaging effect on cells. In "Beneficial Effects of Long-term Endurance Exercise on Leukocyte Telomere Biology," the team measured reliable markers of cell age called telomeres in research subjects. (Telomeres protect the ends of a chromosome from damage. They are longer in younger individuals and gradually shorten as one ages, diminishing their effectiveness.) In the study, measurements from a group of middle-aged runners with a long history of running were compared to those of age-matched, healthy, but inactive subjects. Results indicated a remarkably reduced rate of telomere shortening among the longtime runners versus the physically inactive group, leading to the conclusion that "these findings improve the molecular understanding of beneficial vascular effects of physical activity and implicate an 'anti-aging' effect of physical exercise." In plain English, keep on running!

Colleen De Reuck still is. The four-time Olympian recently won the *masters* division of the Boston Marathon and looks forward to one day "running a marathon with my daughter."

But there's more. A recent study by the Stanford University School of Medicine concluded that regular running increases longevity while decreasing the disabilities common in old age. In "Reduced Disability and Mortality Among Aging Runners," Stanford researchers followed 538 runners and a control group of 423 healthy nonrunners for 21 years. Subjects were aged 50 and above at the start of the research and, consequently, were in their 70s and 80s when the study ended. Findings appeared in a 2008 issue of *Archives of Internal Medicine* and showed that elderly runners presented with significantly fewer disabilities and were half as likely as nonrunners to die early. Their conclusion: "Vigorous exercise (running) at middle and older ages is associated with reduced disability in later life and a notable survival advantage."

Another Stanford study looked at a group of aging runners and found that years of running had not damaged their joints or left them less able to exercise. Runners in their 70s, 80s, and above therefore have no reason to hang up their running shoes, as long as they remain free of illness or serious injury. The general advice for septuagenarian, octogenarian, and nonagenarian runners actually holds true in many respects for younger ones as well; avoidance of overtraining remains critical:

- Make sure to get enough rest. Don't run through an injury.
- Follow a hard day with an easy day. Consider running only every other day.
- Take walk breaks both in races and in regular runs.
- Warm up slowly and for a longer period than before.
- Cross-train, including pool running if available.

Finally, running author John Stanton suggests that having the right frame of mind is also important in a runner's quest to keep running through the ages. "Run by an extended care facility," he says. "Give thanks for your good health, and imagine yourself thinking, focusing, believing, and acting in a more constructive and less anxious way. Then work on replicating this new version of yourself in the real world of life."

RUN TILL YOU'RE 100

It was probably the way he would have wanted it: Jim Fixx breathed his last breath while running. The author of *The Complete Book of Running* and popular exponent of running's health benefits collapsed and died of a heart attack during a run in 1984. Nonrunning skeptics snickered, but others speculated that he would have died years earlier if he had not been a runner. Indeed, doctors later revealed that the cause of his heart attack was not the running but significant blockage of three coronary arteries. A family history of heart disease, a former smoking habit, and elevated cholesterol levels finally caught up with him as they had with his father, who had died at an age 10 years younger than his son. It is almost certain that Jim's years of running enabled him to live a longer and happier life than he would have otherwise.

In the book *Running Until You're 100,* Jeff Galloway writes, "The increased endurance and physical capacity gained from years of running results in a more active lifestyle to the end of your days." He suggests that by balancing several different dimensions—nutrition and exercise, stress and rest, walking and running—runners can control the amount of energy or vitality they experience as they age. "We don't know the year we will leave this earth," he says, "but if you mentally project yourself running into the century mark and make the right adjustments, you'll expect to achieve more vitality during every decade of your life." In other words, runners will be adding not only years to their life but life to those years as well.

Fitness columnist Roy M. Wallack's book *Run for Life* is subtitled "The Anti-aging, Anti-injury, Super Fitness Plan to Keep You Running to 100." He exhorts runners to "not just live to 100, but actively run a 5K, 10K, or even a marathon on your 100th birthday." Frank Levine seems likely to do just that. The masters competitor didn't start running until he was 65, when a friend suggested they run together while his wife was in a nursing home. Since then he has finished 18 marathons and set the American record in the 400-meter dash for men ages 95 to 99.

For many, however, racing *without competing* is the way to prolong running enjoyment. In a *Wall Street Journal* article entitled "Older, Wiser, Slower," six-time Ironman Triathlon winner Mark Allen warns runners, "If you can't let up on the competitive part of it . . . you will grind yourself into the ground and become stressed out, bitter, and unhealthy." How about you? Years from now will you be able to enter a race without caring about your mile splits or your finishing place and still find it as fun and rewarding as before? If so, that can be a victory in itself.

Allen Leigh has the right philosophy. The retired software engineer is the host of the popular blog http://oldmanrunning.org, which "teaches the basics of running via the experiences of a 74-year-old geezer." As he says in an interview posted on the blog, "My running goals are to continue to enjoy my running until I turn over three digits in my age." Are there any secrets for staying motivated to reach that ultimate running goal? Allen thinks so and shares his one-of-a-kind advice exclusively with us in this book:

1. Run because you enjoy it. If you don't enjoy it, don't run. While you're running, think positive thoughts about the people you know. Think of ways you can please them.
2. Unless you're a competitive person, forget speed. Run or walk at a comfortable pace such that you can talk with a running or walking buddy without huffing and puffing.
3. If you run outdoors, enjoy being outside. Stop when you want to admire an animal, flowers, a sunset, or to just to take a break; you're not running to get someplace. If you run on a treadmill in a gym or your home, share your running with a good TV program, DVD, or music.
4. Take satisfaction that even at your age, you can still move and do things besides sit in front of a TV. Take satisfaction that you're a member of a very small group of people who exercise, something that many people much younger than you aren't doing.
5. Enjoy being yourself. Enjoy being free of many of the pressures that surrounded you when you were younger. This is the time of your life when you can live for the sake of living.

Perhaps contributor Bart Yasso puts it best when he says, "Running isn't about how far you go but how far you've come. The reward is living the lifestyle and embracing the journey. It's not only about finishing, it's about moving forward."

ACKNOWLEDGMENTS

This book began simply as a collection of essays on things all runners should do before they die. The suggestions I received in that context from countless runners who share a passion for the sport remain the foundation of this book. My thanks go to all of them.

I was similarly encouraged by the cooperation I received from the elite runners and authors I approached for recommendations and running tips. The enthusiastic and thoughtful responses from those extraordinary athletes and writers became a major component of the book that I will always cherish.

Another elite runner and triathlete, editor Stacy Creamer of Simon & Schuster, realized the potential of this project and became an early advocate of its publication, for which I am grateful. The excitement that she and editor Michelle Howry showed at the outset of this project meant a lot to me. I knew then that "our book," as Michelle put it, was in very capable hands. I appreciate all that they, the designers, the copy editors, and the rest of the Touchstone/Simon & Schuster team did to shepherd this through each step of the publishing process.

Finally, this book would not be possible without the encouragement and commitment of Stephany Evans of FinePrint Literary Management. Her insight brought new dimensions to the book's original concept, and her faith in me and my project is what every author seeks in an agent. She's also a pretty good runner herself.

GOOD GENERAL RUNNING WEB SITES

www.competitiverunner.com provides a myriad of resources for runners, including shoe and book reviews, training advice, race alerts, and a collection of links to other helpful Web sites.

www.coolrunning.com offers an online running log, race pace calculator, racing news, and a special section for beginning runners.

www.letsrun.com surfs the Internet for interesting articles and news about distance running so you don't have to. Its popular message board is a must-read.

www.rrm.com has running news, athlete rankings, all-time performance standards by race distance, and a list of current doping violators.

www.runnersworld.com is a comprehensive site offering advice on training, nutrition, and injury prevention from expert contributors, as well as videos, blogs, a race calendar, and other regular features.

www.runningintheusa.com is an excellent site for races, race results, running clubs, and online forums on everything from nutrition to coping with injuries.

www.runningusa.org is a nonprofit organization and joint venture with USA Track & Field (USATF) to promote and improve the status of road racing in the United States. Among its resources is the State of the Sport Series, which includes results from its annual runner survey and other interesting statistical trends in road racing.

www.runtheplanet.com has information on training, racing, running gear, and finding running routes during your travels.

GOOD WEB SITES FOR WOMEN RUNNERS

www.real-women-running.com is devoted to informing and inspiring women runners and includes testimonials, a free newsletter, and a "Walk to Run" training program among its offerings.

www.runnergirl.com provides a blog along with advice on training, racing, injury prevention, and other resources "to improve the health, fitness, and well-being of girls and women."

www.running-mom.com is for all women runners but also offers specific information to help the transition from woman runner to running mom. Features include a blog, articles about postpartum fitness and running with a stroller, and other resources.

www.runnersworld.com is an excellent site overall and has numerous pages dedicated specifically to women's running.

www.running4women.com is a paid membership site based in the United Kingdom that features downloadable books and training programs and an online forum, and allows members to "Ask the Expert."

www.seemommyrun.com is a nonprofit networking Web portal boasting more than 40,000 members that helps mothers locate or start a running or walking group in their own area.

INDEX

ABOUT THE AUTHOR

CHRIS COOPER has been a runner for most of his life, with numerous road race victories and a sub-three-hour marathon among his achievements. A graduate of Pennsylvania State University, he is host of the blog "Writing on the Run," and has worked in the fields of marketing and public opinion research for more than twenty years. Besides his interests in running and writing, Chris cultivates a passion for wine by working part-time at a local winery. He lives with his wife in West Chester, Pennsylvania.